THE QUICKLY APPROACHING RAPTURE

The Imminent Return of Jesus Christ

Martin W. Sondermann

HISROAD PUBLISHING
Boise, Idaho

The Quickly Approaching Rapture

The Quickly Approaching Rapture: The Imminent Return of Jesus Christ
Copyright © 2020 by Martin W Sondermann,
Hisroad Publishing, Boise, Idaho

All rights reserved. No part of this book may be reproduced or transmitted in any form or by any means without written permission from the author.

ISBN: 9798631941458 (Print Version)

Printed in USA by Hisroad Publishing, Boise, Idaho

The Quickly Approaching Rapture

Dedication

This book is dedicated to those who hold to the Word of God and do not deny His Name!

Table of Contents

Dedication 3
Acknowledgements 5
Preface 9
Introduction 11
Chapter 1: Reasons for This Book 16
Chapter 2: Rapture Defined 29
Chapter 3: Theories and Lenses 44
Chapter 4: The Time of Jacob's Trouble 65
Chapter 5: God's Wrath 73
Chapter 6: Is the Rapture a New Doctrine? 83
Chapter 7: The Imminent Return of Jesus Christ 99
Chapter 8: Spiritual Eyes to See 105
Chapter 9: A Picture of the Rapture 113
Chapter 10: To Disappear or Not Disappear? 129
Chapter 11: Apostasy or Apost-a-see-ya? 140
Chapter 12: The Big Sign 161
Chapter 13: More Signs of the Times 170
Chapter 14: The Quickly Approaching Rapture 189
Chapter 15: Been Left Behind? 215
Study Resources and Contact Information: 230

Acknowledgments

Over the years I have been influenced by so many great men of God. I feel I would be remiss not to at least share with you some of the key people that God has placed in my life, in one way or another, to influence, teach, exhort, and correct me as I have grown in the Lord.

The first man of God that I want to recognize is my own father. He became a believer when I was a young boy, and without his influence and teaching I wouldn't be where I am today. I thank God for both my parents, and for giving me a dad that would share his passion for the Word of God with me.

I also want to thank God for men who have inspired me over the years with their encouragement and their faithful examples. I could never give you every name, but they know who they are, and they include some amazing pastors, teachers, and friends.

As far as those who've had the biggest influence and impact on my Christian life, outside of my own personal circle, the list is long. Most of them are nationally known pastors, teachers and apologists, but I feel it's important to share with you some of those key individuals who have helped me learn about God's Word and aided in my growth as a believer. At the end of this book I am going to include a fairly long list of resources, and all of the following will be included.

Chief among these men would have to Pastor Chuck Smith. It was through his teaching that I was motivated to study the Word of God like never before. He taught us all how to teach the Word simply, simply, simply (you know). It was by his systematic, line-by-line approach that my understanding of the Bible grew in profound ways. Although I was only able to meet Pastor Chuck a handful of times, every interaction with him influenced me greatly. He was always kind to me, and he encouraged me to seek after God with my whole heart. His influence is something that I cherish. That influence was mostly felt through his teachings that he made available through various outlets, but those teachings impacted me in the most life-changing and eternal ways. I will always be grateful to God for the work of Pastor Chuck, and I know if Pastor Chuck were still with us today, he would be the first to give God all the glory! Instead, I trust he is basking in the glory of Jesus at

The Quickly Approaching Rapture

this very moment! After all, Pastor Chuck didn't die he just changed his address.

I also want to thank Pastor Greg Laurie. It was because of his teachings on the radio that I found out about Chuck Smith, and it was Pastor Greg's teachings that taught me, encouraged me, and helped me grow in Christ during a time in my life when it was desperately needed. I still listen to Pastor Greg, and I have, and still recommend his books, radio program, and online teachings to many people.

Other Pastors and teachers that have influenced me through their various ministries over the years include, but are not limited to; Jon Courson, Raul Ries, Charles Stanley, Dr. Ed Hindson, Adrian Rogers, Skip Heitzig, Mike Macintosh, Don Stewart, Ken Graves, J. Vernon McGee, Ravi Zacharias, Jack Hibbs, Ray Comfort, Pancho Juarez, Alistair Begg, and Dr. David Jeremiah, just to name a few.

I also want to note that I'm am not blaming any of the above influences for my work! I don't expect them to agree with 100 percent of what I have written, but I do want to credit each one of them for the influence they have had in my life and thank them for being faithful to their calling. Their various books, television broadcasts, online videos, and radio programs have been a huge blessing! I

The Quickly Approaching Rapture

have learned so much from them, and I felt it was important to include them so the reader can understand my biblical influences outside of my "official" education.

Preface

Before diving into the topic of this book I want to give the reader my standard word of caution. This is something I want to include with every book I write. First, do not blindly trust or accept the opinions, thoughts, and understanding of doctrine, theology, or eschatology presented within these pages, or within any pages outside of the Holy Scriptures. What I want to challenge each individual to do is to simply do what the Scripture states in 1 Thessalonians chapter 5 verse 21, *"Test all things; hold fast what is good."* **(NKJ)** The Bible also instructs us in 2 Timothy 2:15 to, *"Study to show thyself approved unto God, a workman that needeth not to be ashamed, rightly dividing the Word of Truth." (KJV)* This is the standard that all believers should follow, and I for one will not be offended if you think I have fallen off my proverbial rocker. I simply ask that you let me know where you believe I have erred according to the Scriptures. Also, please know this book is not being written to be different,

The Quickly Approaching Rapture

take a contrary view for contrary's sake, argue, or try to prove to you I have some kind of superior intelligence or secret knowledge. This book comes from the heart of someone who loves to study God's Word, and very much enjoys sharing what he learns with believers and non-believers alike.

Introduction

Some Personal Motivation

I felt it was also important to include a personal motivation for writing books like this. To do so I must start with an event that might help you understand what motivates me to write and to share my faith. It begins at a Bible conference in the early 2000's in Meridian, Idaho. This is when I realized God was calling me to step out of my comfort zone, and to step up to teach His Word. And, although I failed the test that day, what happened during that conference changed my life forever.

Dr. Chuck Missler was speaking during an amazing conference back in the early 2000's. During his presentation my heart began to beat hard in my chest. I felt like my temperature was elevating, and God began to speak to me. It wasn't an audible voice, or even a voice that I could hear in my own mind. Instead it was like a lot of information just filled my mind. God instantly let me know that He was calling me to teach His Word. But my fear immediately

The Quickly Approaching Rapture

took over. You see, one of my biggest fears in life was standing up in front of people to speak, or really to do anything personal in front of a large crowd. The crazy thing is that I could play sports in front of any size crowd, and it never bothered me. I could also sit with a small group and share and read, and that never bothered me. However, for some reason I was petrified of standing in front of an audience giving a speech or lecture. I would rather run away and hide than stand in front of people in naked humility. I later realized that this was oppression sent from the enemy, and it was also deeply rooted in my own pride, but that day at the conference I was far away from that understanding.

While Dr. Missler was teaching I could feel the presence of the Holy Spirit in a way I had never felt before. I knew God was calling me, and He was also telling me that He was about to prove His calling. He immediately showed me that He was going to have Dr. Missler stop his presentation just to acknowledge me. My reaction in my mind was, "What!? No, please no!" I don't know how I understood it, but it was as clear as any message I had ever received. I panicked and I almost left the crowded room. However, I was frozen in fear. My heart began to beat faster and faster, and I could feel it pounding in my chest. I was overwhelmed by something I had never experienced. I kept looking down at the ground because I didn't want to look at Dr. Missler. I knew what was coming. It was the only time in my life anything like this had ever happened, and I will never forget it.

A few moments after all of this began, sure enough, Dr. Missler stopped. He then addressed the crowd and said God had spoken to him and He needed to acknowledge someone in the room (there were hundreds of us there). He said that God had shown him that this person, whoever they were, had been called by God to do something for the Kingdom within the next six months. I sank back in my chair because I knew it was me. Again, I was frozen. He then said that whoever this person was, God wanted them to stand up and acknowledge their calling. He said that God wanted him to pray for this person, and pray as a group, but again, I sat frozen. There was no way I was standing up to be the center of attention.

After what seemed like an eternity, one guy stood up sheepishly, and then one more. Dr. Missler looked right at me, and I knew I was disobeying God, and I knew I was being a coward. I knew what God was calling me to do, but I was frozen in fear.

After a few minutes Dr. Missler prayed for the guys who stood up, but I could tell that he wasn't satisfied with what had transpired. His encouragement sounded like he knew the person who God wanted to stand up didn't stand. Proof of this was what God had done in my heart and mind before he even paused his teaching. I knew for a fact it was me, and I had failed.

I left that conference that day broken. I knew I had let God down. I knew that I had been so cowardly. However, within a few weeks God encouraged me greatly through His Word. I begged Him to help me be stronger, and to not be afraid. At that point He gave me a new life verse which was 2 Timothy 1:7; ***"For God hath not given us the spirit of fear; but of power, and of love, and of a sound mind." (KJV).***

Not long after the conference, and my failure, I preached my very first Sermon! My text was Genesis 22, and I taught the whole chapter. While I was frozen in fear and petrified to stand up in front of the crowd at the conference, God encouraged me and helped me to have

The Quickly Approaching Rapture

victory in my defeat. He built me up and gave me the strength to stand in front of others and to share His Word.

That failure at Dr. Missler's conference haunted me for a while, but then God used it in a profound way in my life. His voice was so clear that day, and I failed to do what He asked me to do. It was one of the worst feelings I have ever had in my life. However, that experience, on that day, has helped me so much over the years. That same experience is what has helped me to have the courage to write books that I believe He is calling me to write. I never want to stay frozen again.

Chapter 1

Reasons for This Book

Primary Motivation

I sincerely believe God has called me to write this book for such a time as this. I want you to know that I feel a quickening in my spirit regarding the Lord coming for His Church. For a while now God has been opening my eyes in a much clearer way to the days in which we live. While I have always believed the Rapture could be at any moment, I truly and sincerely believe it is coming very soon! In Matthew 24:46 we read, *"Blessed is that servant, whom his lord when he cometh shall find so doing."*

In saying that, this book is written to three groups of people. First, the faithful Church, second those who think they are Christians but may not be, or may be living a compromised life, and lastly to everyone else.

The Faithful Church

To the faithful Church I say hold on! Keep serving Jesus as we see that Day approaching (Heb 10:25). He will be here soon, so do all you can to preach the Gospel and make disciples. Let's take as many people up with us as we can!

However, I bring a warning to those in the Church who aren't living the way God wants them to. In 1 John 2:28 we see a powerful verse relating to being ready for the time when Jesus comes for His Church. It is written, ***"And now, little children, abide in him; that, when he shall appear, we may have confidence, and <u>not be ashamed before him at his coming</u>."***

Do you want to be ashamed at His coming? I don't. Wouldn't you rather be the one who is whole heartily serving the Lord when He arrives? I know I do, and let's face it folks, we have wasted enough time on our own things, the worries of this world, and on things that just won't matter eternally. 1 Peter 4:7 states, ***"But the end of all things is at hand: be ye therefore sober and watch unto prayer."***

Christian By Name Only

To those who claim to be Christians but may, in fact, be lying to themselves, I say, wake up before it's too late! The real challenge is that most of those in this camp don't know they aren't saved. Some prayed a single prayer and think they are good to go. Some have served in church for years, and yet their hearts are far from God. This is not something I say to claim the moral high ground or to look down on anyone. I just know that in Matthew Chapter 7 Jesus tells us that there will be a whole group of people who claim to have done many wonderful works in "His" name, and Jesus is going to say to them, *"Depart from me I never knew you"* (Mat 7:23).

Ten Virgins

We also see in Matthew 25 a story of ten virgins. Jesus says that five of them were *"foolish"* but five were *"wise."* The five foolish didn't have oil for their lamps when the *"bridegroom"* showed up. However, the <u>five wise virgins did have oil</u> in their lamps. At midnight when the call came to rise up and go, those foolish virgins were, in essence, left behind. Why? No oil in their lamps. The foolish tried to get the oil from the wise, but there was only enough oil for the wise. As you go read this story yourself in Matthew 25 remember that in the Scriptures "oil" is often a picture of the Holy Spirit.

What I believe, and I am certainly not alone in this, is that Jesus was saying that there are some among us who think themselves ready for the bridegroom, but they are not ready. They don't have oil. Sure, they know <u>about</u> Jesus,

The Quickly Approaching Rapture

and <u>about</u> His Church, some of them even know <u>about</u> the Bible and serving others, but they are not born again! They don't have the oil. They are not regenerated and filled with the Spirit of God (Rom 8:9-11). This is extremely scary, and this book will challenge everyone to look deeper at their faith, especially in the times we live where the signs are all around that Jesus will be here very soon for His Church. But know this, He will only take those with the oil.

The Non-Believer

To those who have yet placed their trust in Jesus Christ my prayer is that this book would point you to the King of Kings and the Lord of Lords. He bore all of your sins on the Cross, and He stands ready to receive those who surrender their lives to His free gift of Grace provided by His precious Blood and Sacrifice. It has been said that "All roads lead to God" and this is true. All roads do lead to God, <u>but</u> all roads do not lead to Heaven!

Every person will stand in front of God one day, and Scripture says that every knee will bow, and every tongue will confess, that Jesus Christ is Lord (Rom 14:11, Phil 2:10-11). However, it matters on which side of eternity YOU confess. If you confess Him on this side of eternity and on this side of the Rapture, you will be taken up and be

The Quickly Approaching Rapture

received by Jesus before the great and terrible time known as the Tribulation begins. If you reject the free Gift of Salvation though Christ by Grace alone, then you will have to endure the worst time this world has ever known. Not only that, but if you die in that condition, you will spend an eternity separated from God in a real place called Hell. Jesus taught more about Hell than He did of Heaven, and just because you don't believe in it doesn't mean it isn't real.

My hope is that by the time you are done reading this book, you will be able to recognize that Jesus is The Creator and the very One who gave you life. He is the One who took your sins upon Himself at the Cross so that you might be with Him forever. The Gospel is simple, and it takes a good theologian to mess it up. We are saved by God's Grace alone through faith and it's not by works (Eph 2:8-9). Your works can't save you. No one is good enough. But just know, that everyone who calls upon the name of Jesus will be saved (Rom 10:13) and that whosoever believes in Him shall have everlasting life (John 3:16). But, as previously noted, it takes an honest surrender because many who call themselves "believers" will be cast out.

The Quickly Approaching Rapture

I beg you to get honest with the Lord while you still can! Give your life to Him while there is still time. No one is guaranteed another day or another moment. The time to surrender is now. He is coming back soon!

To the Critic

I believe the Rapture is something that should comfort and motivate all believers! I also know that I shouldn't be surprised by the denial of the Rapture by some. After all, in 2 Peter 3:3-4 we read, *"Knowing this first, that there shall come in the last days scoffers, walking after their own lusts, And saying, Where is the promise of his coming? for since the fathers fell asleep, all things continue as they were from the beginning of the creation."* [i]

To those reading this book that don't believe in a Rapture or who scoff at us who do, I just ask that you read this book with *"readiness of mind"* (Acts 17:11). I am not asking you to blindly trust or believe. I am challenging you to study out the things I bring to the table. For those who are believers, just know, you have a responsibility to either test and prove the things I have written, or to correct me if you feel I have erred. I am not claiming to know all that there is to know about the Rapture, but I believe it is clearly taught in Scripture, and I am putting the evidence I have found out there for examination. And please know, my heart is to share what I have learned in a responsible way knowing that teachers will be held to a higher standard of judgment (James 3:1).

A Trend

Another motivating factor behind writing this book is a trend I have noticed lately. This trend, which can only be described as a denial of the Rapture <u>within</u> the Christian Church, has expanded greatly. Over the last decade it seems to me that some who once believed in a Rapture now reject it. Related to this topic is a growing number within the Body of Christ who also teach that Christians will have to go through the Tribulation. In my experience some who are propagating such a teaching are also trying to sell prepper supplies or books or DVD's. Others who teach this seem to relish the thought of living like Mad Max in a post-apocalyptic world. Still, I have spoken with a few who sincerely believe the Bible says that we as believers will go through part, or all, of the Tribulation. My hope is that this book will change your mind, or at the very least, it will give you some hope.

The Quickly Approaching Rapture

We Will Experience Challenging Times

I am going to pause for just a moment to also say there is nothing wrong with being ready for hard times. There is certainly nothing wrong with making sure your family has enough during a crisis. I say this because even though I don't believe Christians will go through the "Tribulation" I do believe times are going to become increasingly difficult in this world, and Christians would be wise to prepare. After all, in times of crisis the Church should shine! We could be a very effective witness in the coming challenging years. So, prep away! Buy your supplies, grow your gardens, stockpile your needs, but make sure you don't make the focus only you. This world needs the message we have, and that will be especially noticeable in the trying times to come.

But know this, even though we as believers will have to endure the wrath of the enemy at times, or even the wrath of man, we will never have to endure the wrath of God. While the time leading up to the Tribulation will be full of the former, the wrath of God will not occur until His Church is removed. In other words, Christians can expect things on this planet to get worse before they get better for us. I don't mean to rain on anyone's parade, but I also

The Quickly Approaching Rapture

know A.W. Tozer once said something along the lines that a problem within Christianity is that too many Christians treat the world like a playground rather than a battleground. In the coming days I believe Christians will endure difficulty at times. It won't be comparable to the Tribulation, but it may cause some to wander while it will cause others to seek God like never before. I hope and pray all of us will begin to seek the Lord in these days in purposeful and profound ways.

The Darby Excuse

Those who reject the doctrine of the Rapture often point to a man named John Nelson Darby. He was a Pastor who lived in the nineteenth century and is often accused of being the person who invented this "idea". They claim it was something he made up and is without Biblical support. To be fair, those same critics usually credit a few others as well, but Darby is most often premier among those they blame. In this book I will attempt to prove to you that this is just not true. This book will look at Scripture carefully to see what it says concerning this thing called the Rapture, and it will look at early teachings in the Church that support a Rapture viewpoint.

The Quickly Approaching Rapture

You Just Want to Escape

Another motivation for writing this book is a response to those who claim that people who believe in the Rapture are "escapists" who care nothing about the present time and the world we live in. These same critics claim it's dangerous to live focused on heavenly things and not taking care of earthly matters. Many critics also accuse those who believe in the Rapture as "over-spiritualizing" the Bible or seeing things in the passages that just aren't there. This book will show why this isn't true, but why some of those same critics may be doing exactly the opposite of that which they accuse Rapture adherents of doing. Namely, they are too focused on this world, they themselves are "under-spiritualizing" Scripture, and they just fail to see things within the Scripture that seem to be so clear.

The Imminent Return of Jesus

While some claim that the Church has no history of the Rapture as a doctrine, or that it's made up or fantasy, I would respond by saying that Scripture clearly points to the "imminent return of Christ". You see, throughout the Bible there are passages that speak of Christ coming at any moment. There are also several passages that point to several events having to happen before Christ returns to this earth to set up His Kingdom? So, which is it? I tell you it's both! Just as many in the first century didn't realize Jesus would have a second coming to this planet, and that His first season here would be to atone for the sins of the world, many in this day, fail to recognize that Scripture clearly teaches Jesus will come once <u>for</u> His Church and then return <u>with</u> His Church to set up His Kingdom. This will be covered in greater detail later in this book.

Seven Letters to Seven Churches

We will also look at some curious passages in Revelation relating to the Seven Letters to the Seven Churches in an effort to gauge what is coming and who will be taken. These seven letters appear to have a promise to four historical churches, as it relates to the Rapture, and whether or not those within those churches will be taken or left behind.

Will Christians Disappear?

This book will also look at the traditional teaching that all Christians will disappear at the moment of the Rapture. I will examine certain passages in Scripture that seem to be saying a second option could be possible. Instead of disappearing, could it be that all Christians will simply leave their bodies behind? In other words, will the Rapture look like a massive number of deaths or the largest case of missing persons in human history? Will those who have went on before us, who are with the Lord now, receive bodies made from their old flesh at the Rapture, or will they be given brand-new bodies all together?

The Last Days

Additionally, I recognize that we are in the last of the last days. Not just the last days, but I believe we are in the "last-of-the-last" days, if that makes sense? This book will examine several things that point to the soon return of Jesus Christ for His Church. And, whether you think that's important or not, I want you to know it really is. Because, all of us, if we are honest, have things in our lives we need to correct. Beyond that, most, if not all of us, have loved ones who are not saved, and this can help to motivate us to be much bolder in sharing the Gospel.

Warning

To the reader I do feel I should warn you. I believe the Bible has many themes and lessons that repeat over and over. This is because you and I need to hear something over and over to learn. This has helped me in my own studies of Scripture, but I wanted to warn you that I will repeat many

The Quickly Approaching Rapture

passages of Scripture within this book. This is in an effort to give you evidence and to help you remember what you have read.

Chapter 2

Rapture Defined

But, the Word Rapture Isn't in the Bible

When studying the Bible concerning the topic of the Rapture it doesn't take long for the average Christian to realize that the word "Rapture" isn't found in the Bible. With today's modern computer/phone/tablet and online Bible tools available, it's really a matter of seconds that this can be discovered. However, while the word "Rapture" isn't found in the Holy Scriptures, at least in any of the standard English Translations, it doesn't mean a word meaning the same thing isn't found somewhere in the Book. Also, simply because the word "Rapture" isn't found it doesn't mean the doctrine can't be found. Take for instance the word "Trinity". This word isn't found in a common English translation either, but any Christian with foundational understandings about our faith certainly recognizes that the doctrine of the Trinity is displayed within the passages of the Bible. It's only when a person studies out the various passages, that share truth about the Trinity, that this doctrine is revealed through a gathering of information and an assembly of verses from Scripture into one coherent model.

For those who don't know, or for those who need a refresher, the way to interpret Scripture is called Hermeneutics. It's a logical way to look at the text, compare and contrast it, and incorporate spiritual understandings and practical applications. This is the only way to come to a better understanding of many things in Scripture like the Trinity.

Another very important thing to remember whenever we study the Bible is that while the Bible is a book penned by men we must always remember it was inspired by God. In 2 Timothy 3:16 the Bible states, ***"All scripture is given by <u>inspiration of God</u>, and is profitable for doctrine, for reproof, for correction, for instruction in righteousness"***. The phrase *"inspiration of God"* is literally "Theopneustos" in the Greek. This means "God to breathe", in other words, the Bible is "God breathed". I often tell people if they have never heard God speak to them to simply open the Bible and read it out loud. It's all God's Word! Yes, He used men to write His message down, but it's still His message, and that same passage in 2 Timothy states that ALL Scripture was given this way.

The Quickly Approaching Rapture

Now, if you want to debate the topic of which books of the Bible should be included in the Bible, that topic will have to wait. A quick note about that is this; if God is who He says He is, then protecting the books He wanted us to have in the Bible is very simple for Him.

Jumping back to the subject of the Bible and proper interpretation we must understand that because the Bible has natural and spiritual understandings it requires a different kind of interpretation than a book simply imagined and written by men. In a book I highly recommend, *Introduction to Biblical Hermeneutics: The Search for Meaning*, Walter C. Kaiser Jr. Explains that hermeneutics is needed, not simply because the Bible is "divine" in its origin, but because the Bible is also a 'human book'."[ii]

In much the way the "Logos" (John 1), the Word Made Flesh, Jesus Himself was fully human and fully divine. The Bible has a similar aspect to it. But, before I go too far on this, I also want to point out that we as Christians do not worship "Father, Son and Holy Bible" we worship the Trinity, "Father, Son, and Holy Spirit". We don't worship the Bible, but again, we must acknowledge that the Bible is a book that is "God breathed" (2 Tim 3:16). It is the very Word of God, and as such, it should be treated in a way that recognizes this fact.

In saying that, I jump back to the previous point, proper hermeneutics is needed to balance the human and divine nature of His Word. It also requires the Holy Spirit within a believer to understand what you are reading because we know that the *"natural"*, or unsaved person, can't truly understand what they are reading (1 Cor 2:14). Can God reveal Himself to a non-believer through His Word? Of course, He can, but that's done with God's intervention and completely aligned with His sovereignty.

Doctrines like the previously mentioned Trinity do not come from one single verse. We as Christians know the Trinity is true, but the only way to come to that understanding is by studying several passages that reveal this powerful single truth. In other words, we allow verses to build upon each other utilizing a proper and sound hermeneutic. This can also be said when it comes to the doctrine of the Rapture.

The Word Rapture

Now, as far as the word "Rapture" not being found in most English translations of the Bible, this is simply because it isn't derived from an English word. The word

The Quickly Approaching Rapture

"Rapture" actually comes from the Latin word "Rapiemur" which is found in the Latin Vulgate, which is a Latin translation of the Holy Scriptures. In that translation the famous passage concerning the Rapture found in 1 Thessalonians 4:17 displays this word. That verse in English reads, *"Then we which are alive and remain shall be <u>caught up</u> together with them in the clouds, to meet the Lord in the air: and so shall we ever be with the Lord."*

In the Greek texts of the Bible the words *"caught up"* is the single word "Harpazo", and it's pronounced har-pad'-zo. According to *Strong's Bible Concordance* (G726) it is a word which means to "seize" or to "catch away up" to "pluck" to "pull" or to "take" which is implied "by force". *Strong's* further explains that this word is derived from another Greek word which is "Aihreomai" pronounced hahee-reh'-om-ahee, which means "to take for oneself" or to "prefer".

When using those previously mentioned Bible computer tools, we find this word "Harpazo" is used 13 times in Scripture. I feel I would be doing the reader an injustice by not looking at each of these, at least briefly.

In the book of Matthew "Harpazo" is used twice, once in chapter 11 and once in chapter 13. In chapter 11 it is found in verse 12 when it states, *"And from the days of John the Baptist until now the kingdom of heaven suffereth violence, and the violent take it by force"* (KJV). The words there *"take it by force"* is the single word "Harpazo".

Before I jump too much further, I feel I must reiterate that I do not support the use of any single verse of Scripture for the creation of any doctrine, theology, or even an opinion. I think any passage that is quoted or studied must be taken in full context. For the sake of this study when looking at a single verse it is done so to provide the use of the single word, "Harpazo", and it is not to give a full and complete context of the verse, but rather, a full and complete context of the use of the single word. In saying that, I will do my best to give context as it applies, but please feel free to do this yourself if you feel more is needed or if you believe that I have taken anything out of its proper context.

Going back to that verse in Matthew, the word "Harpazo" is found in the phrase *"take it by force"*, which is exactly what it means in that verse. In Matthew 13:19 we see that "Harpazo" is then used as a word to describe the actions of *"the wicked one"*. It states, *"When *any one heareth the word of the kingdom, and understandeth it not, then cometh the wicked one, and <u>catcheth away</u> that which was sown in his heart. This is he which received seed by the wayside."* Here we see that the phrase *"catcheth away"* or to "catch away" means exactly what it says it does. Something is caught away or taken away.

Are you seeing an early pattern?

In the book of John, the word "Harpazo" is used four times. The first usage is found in 6:15 when Jesus *"perceived that they would "come and <u>take Him by force</u>"*. Again, it means to literally take Him by force. In chapter 10 verse 12 a couple of evil creatures are described. This time it's a fake shepherd who's in it for the money and who runs away when the wolf comes. It reads, *"But he that is a hireling, and not the shepherd, whose own the sheep are not, seeth the wolf coming, and leaveth the sheep, and fleeth: and the wolf <u>catcheth</u> them, and scattereth the sheep."* Here the word "Harpazo" is used in a way that means to "catch".

In John 10:28-29 we see the last two usages of the word in this book. In both cases the word in English is pluck and both are good news for believers. I will start the quote with verse 27 in which Jesus says, *"My sheep hear my voice, and I know them, and they follow me."* He then adds, *"And I give unto them eternal life; and they shall never perish, neither shall any man <u>pluck</u> them out of my hand. My Father, which gave them me, is greater than all; and no man is able to <u>pluck</u> them out of my Father's hand."* (V.28-29).

The usage of "Harpazo" in these two verses explains that if you belong to Jesus there is no one that can "Harpazo", or pluck, or take, or snatch away, or pull, or take by force, any of us who belong to Him! I won't jump off track here, but please know, if you are a true believer in Christ, born again, with the Spirit of God living in you (Rom.8:9-11) you are secure. It is God who keeps you and no one can pluck you out of His hand.

Continuing, there are two uses of "Harpazo" in the book of Acts and an equal number in 2 Corinthians. Acts 8:39 is fascinating. It involves a disciple named Philip. The Bible states that an Angel of the Lord spoke to Philip and told him to get up and go toward the south, *"unto Gaza"*, from Jerusalem, which the Bible says was desert land. So, Philip was obedient and went. Once arriving Philip sees a man who is from Ethiopia. In fact, the Bible states that this

The Quickly Approaching Rapture

man was a, *"eunuch of great authority under Candace queen of the Ethiopians"* and it goes on to say that this eunuch, *"had charge of all her treasure, and had come to Jerusalem for to worship"* (V.27). The Spirit of God told Philip to go to the eunuch's chariot. Philip did just that. When he approached the man, the Bible says he could hear him reading from *"Esaias the prophet"* (V.30). Verses 32-33 states, *"The place of the scripture which he read was this, He was led as a sheep to the slaughter; and like a lamb dumb before his shearer, so opened he not his mouth: In his humiliation his judgment was taken away: and who shall declare his generation? for his life is taken from the earth."*

Philip then explains to the eunuch of who that Scripture was speaking about and continues to give the Ethiopian the Gospel message of Jesus Christ.

Here's where it gets crazy.

The man receives Christ and is baptized, but as soon as the baptism is complete something happens to Philip. He's raptured! Okay, well at least he is harpazoed! If that's even a word. Verse 39 says, *"And when they were come up out of the water, the Spirit of the Lord <u>caught</u>*

The Quickly Approaching Rapture

away *Philip, that the eunuch saw him no more: and he went on his way rejoicing."*

Two things stand out in this verse. First, Philip disappears and the Ethiopian just *"went on his way rejoicing."* That's just so funny and awesome to me. A guy shows up, teaches him the Gospel, baptizes him and then vanishes. No problem, I'm just happy to be saved!

Another thing that is fascinating is that Philip was then *"found at Azotus"* which is the ancient city of Ashdod. Which means that Philip was taken from Gaza to Ashdod in a supernatural way seemingly instantaneously. That is about 19 miles from my calculations and it's just incredible. And what word was used to describe this supernatural journey of Philip? It was "Harpazo". In English it was *"caught away"*.

In Acts 23 we see another usage of "Harpazo". In this passage Paul was in danger of being killed and the *"chief captain"* instructs his soldiers to go and *"take him by force"* (v.10), speaking of Paul. That phase is "Harpazo".

Another passage relating to the Apostle Paul is found in 2 Corinthians 12:2 and 12:4. In these two verses we read the description of some kind of experience *"a man"* had. Most people who study this kind of thing, at least that I know, think Paul is speaking about himself but not wanting to draw attention to himself. In other words, it was Paul sincerely trying to be humble. Nevertheless, in this experience Paul describes a journey to the *"third heaven"*. For those who don't know the Bible speaks about three heavens. First, the sky where the birds and clouds fly and float. The second heaven is outer space. The third heaven is Heaven itself. The place where God's Throne is. In any case, Paul talks about this journey *"a man"* had to the *"third heaven"*. How did that man get there? Paul goes on to explains twice that this man was *"caught up"* or "Harpazo".

In the previously mentioned famous passage of the Rapture in 1 Thessalonians 4:17 we recognize what is being said. It states that those who are, *"alive and remain"* will be *"caught up"* or "Harpazo" in the Greek.

In Jude verse 23 it is written, ***"And others save with fear, <u>pulling</u> them out of the fire; hating even the garment spotted by the flesh."*** I once heard a pastor years ago say that the Gospel can love you into the Kingdom of God or scare you into the Kingdom. Another pastor said that the Bible is a message that comforts the afflicted and afflicts the comfortable. Here in Jude we see there are some who are saved by the message of Grace, that their sins have been paid for by Jesus and it's a free gift, but that others are saved because they recognize the reality of Hell. In this context they are pulled out of the fire. That word for *"pulling"* is "Harpazpo".

The last verse in the Bible which uses the word "Harpazo" is found in the book of Revelation. In Chapter 12 of this amazing book we read about a great *"wonder in heaven"* which is *"a woman clothed with the sun, and the moon under her feet"* and she also has a crown of *"twelve stars"* upon her head.

A side note about the book of Revelation, is that the signs and symbols in that book can be explained by allowing Scripture to interpret Scripture (Hermeneutics). What I mean by this is that all the strange signs and symbols of Revelation are explained elsewhere in the Bible. Of course, there are some exceptions. When the book says something is "like" something, then the obvious is being displayed. It simply means it is "like" something. But, as far as the key signs and symbols in Revelation, those are displayed elsewhere in Scripture and this is how we understand what they mean. In an effort to understand

The Quickly Approaching Rapture

Revelation a person must be willing to search the Bible for the key to understanding each sign or symbol. In Revelation 12 this woman who is described can be understood as the nation of Israel, and before you tune out please know, this is very important for our context, so stick with me.

In Genesis 37 we see the key to understanding the Revelation 12 passage. Genesis 37:9 states, *"And he dreamed yet another dream, and told it his brethren, and said, Behold, I have dreamed a dream more; and, behold, the sun and the moon and the eleven stars made obeisance to me."*

The person having the dream is Joseph, and he sees the sun, moon and eleven stars bowing down to him. Joseph then shares his dream with his family, to which his brothers understand that this dream meant that Joseph's mom, dad, and brothers would be somehow bowing to Joseph and they aren't happy about it. But, it had greater meaning than just that. And, before you reject this because there are only *"eleven stars"* and the passage in Revelation has *"twelve stars"*, just know, Joseph is the twelfth star. After all, who is Joseph's dad? It's Jacob, who is also

The Quickly Approaching Rapture

known as Israel. Who are Joseph's brothers? They are the origin of the Tribes of Israel.

So, if we understand that this passage in Genesis 37 is pointing to Revelation and this is the same symbolism representing Israel, who then is the *"Man Child"* it is speaking about in Revelation 12:5? It states, *"And she brought forth a man child, who was to rule all nations with a rod of iron: and her child was <u>caught up</u> unto God, and to his throne."*

In context it is easy to understand that the Bible is speaking of Jesus here. He was born of a Jewish Virgin, and we know Jesus was of the Tribe of Judah and in the line of David. So, when it speaks of the *"woman"* clothed in the sun, moon and twelve stars, it is saying that *"she"* brought forth a *"man child who was to rule all nations with a rod on iron"* we know it can only be speaking of Jesus being brought forth through the nation of Israel.

But, how was Jesus *"caught up"* which is the word "Harpazo"? In Acts Chapter 1 we get the answer as we read about how Jesus ascended into Heaven after His resurrection. Those watching Jesus ascend were then spoken to by *"two men"* in *"white apparel"* (V.10) who told them, *"Ye men of Galilee, why stand ye gazing up*

The Quickly Approaching Rapture

into heaven? this same Jesus, which is taken up from you into heaven, <u>shall so come in like manner as ye have seen him go into heaven</u>" (V.11).

Back to Revelation 12:5 we get a further description of how Jesus ascended into Heaven in that, he was *"caught up"* or "Harpazo". Also, the verse in Acts tells us that Jesus will come back *"in like manner as ye have seen him go into heaven."* Jesus was "caught up" and when He comes back for His Church He is going to do the very thing with them.

Chapter 3

Theories and Lenses

Pre, Mid, Post, Pan?

When studying the rapture of the Church it's important to recognize that there are many different theories on the event, its purpose, and its timing. This book will look at the four most common theories as it relates to the rapture, but I will also touch on a couple less-known theories. The four main theories will be the Pre-Tribulation, Mid-Tribulation, Pre-Wrath and Post-Tribulation theories respectively.

However, there is an often-used term, that those who use it, usually do so to sound witty or seemingly humble. They say they are "Pan-Tribulation", which simply means they will just see how it all "pans" out. In most cases, I have found, that those who use this term are not really interested in the Bible in the way they should be as Christians. While that is painting with a broad brush, I am sorry to say, it is very often true. Now, there are certainly those who just haven't come to a sincere conclusion about

The Quickly Approaching Rapture

the timing of the Rapture, and that becomes evident as you talk with them, but the vast majority of those who say they are "Pan-Trib" are the former, in my opinion. Those who use this term "Pan-Trib" often fail to recognize a few things. First, we are commanded to study the Word of God as workmen who won't be ashamed (2 Tim 2:15). Also, a careful study of the topic can reveal basic truths about it. The Bible has plenty to say about it, and surely God wouldn't leave us in the dark. After all, doesn't the passage that explains that Jesus will come like a thief in the night in 1 Thessalonians 5:2 then also say in verse 4, *"But ye, brethren, are not in darkness, that that day should overtake you as a thief."*

Lastly, we are to be those who are looking for His coming (Heb 9:28), and not those who simply wait to see how it all pans out. In fact, the word used in that verse in Hebrews is "Apekdechomai" which Strong's says means, "to expect fully" or to "wait for" (G553).

Needless to say, it's frustrating for me when I hear this "Pan-Trib" phrase being thrown out there. If you are one who has sincerely studied this topic, or if you are one who has ignored it, my hope is that this book will help you. If you are a "Pan-Trib" theorist after reading, I guess we will just agree to disagree and keep loving each other as brothers and sisters in Christ—but please expect an eyeroll.

"Do you feel better after your rant?" You ask.

"Actually, I do, thank you!"

No Rapture

Now, before jumping into the various other terms used to describe the timing of the Rapture, I want to address those who do not believe in the Rapture in any way, shape, or form. I'm not going to spend too much time on this, but just know any group, church, person, teacher or movement, that teaches that there is no Rapture, or that we as the Church will somehow usher in the Kingdom of Christ, I encourage you to avoid them. If you don't understand why I say this now, my hope is that by the end of this book you will.

We Are Still Family

I also want you to know I am not saying those who do not believe in a Rapture can't be saved. There are many who are currently saved. However, I do think what a person believes about the Rapture says a lot about their understanding of Scripture as a whole. I sincerely want people to study their Bibles in a way that is systematic and helps them to have the ability to allow Scripture to interpret Scripture rather than trusting what a commentary says or a teacher explains. Yes, we need teachers in the Church (Eph 4:11), but we also need students willing to search the Scriptures like the Bereans in Acts 17. They received Paul's message but then tested it with Scripture. This is how each of us should be. As I mentioned early in this book, that's how you should be with everything I write as well. Test all things! Hold to the things that are proven and true. In the end, we as true believers are still family, even if some of our family members don't agree with us. The Rapture isn't a salvation issue. After all, *"For by grace are ye saved through faith; and that not of yourselves: it is the gift of God: Not of works, lest any man should boast"* (Eph 2:8).

Speaking of Those That Don't Agree

One viewpoint that is related to a "No Rapture" stance is called "Amillennial". Those who hold to this viewpoint do not believe in a tribulation period the same way those who hold to a pre, mid, or even many who hold a post-tribulation theory. And, while some in the Amillennial camp believe in a kind-of, sort-of, something that might look like a "rapture" at the return of Jesus, most do not believe in the Rapture at all. I am careful not to put all Amillennial folks into one camp because of my interaction with so many and their viewpoints have varied. However, one thing is for sure the Amillennial view doesn't allow a Rapture and then a literal thousand-year reign of Christ on Earth. This is because this theory teaches that the millennial reign of Jesus is not a future event that will take place for one-thousand literal years, but instead, it started at His ascension and will complete at His return with no literal span of time. In his book *Things to Come: A Study in Biblical Eschatology*, Dwight J. Pentecost explains the difference between the Amillennial and Premillennial and Pre-Tribulation and Post-Tribulation viewpoints. He notes that it is certainly "hermeneutical", and it stems from the "adoption of divergent and irreconcilable methods of interpretation."[iii] He further explains that the biggest factor separating these groups is that the Premillennial camp holds to an "emphasis" on "literal interpretation of Scripture".[iv] A further explanation of this would be that the Amillennial view interprets most of the prophetic passages found in the Book of Revelation and elsewhere in Scripture as "symbolic" and not "literal." Whereas, those who hold to a

The Quickly Approaching Rapture

Premillennial view look to interpret Scripture as literal unless it is used in a clearly symbolic way.

Three Most Common Lenses

To further understand this, I feel I must address the three basic camps of interpretation when it comes to prophetic end-times events within Protestant/Evangelical churches before giving you the four Rapture viewpoints. These three "camps" are not to be confused with the different theories of the Rapture itself, as they have similar names, but instead these are more understood as the lens in which, various Christian groups, denominations, theologians, and scholars view the Scripture, prophecy, and thus, the Rapture. This is very important because the lens an individual person or a denomination chooses to utilize to view Scripture through, will determine their hermeneutics, and it's basically the foundation upon which each builds its understanding.

When I get to Heaven, I think one of the questions I would like to ask is why God allowed different lenses within Christianity. Okay, probably not. I'm sure questions like this will evaporate instantly in the presence of our Great God and Savior, Jesus Christ! But it is amazing to me that people who believe in the same Lord can see things so differently.

Amillennial Lens

As mentioned, there are those who hold to an "Amillennial" viewpoint. By their name Amillennial, which means basically means "No Millennium" tells you that they don't believe in a Millennium. Or at least, what most of us would call a Millennium. To be fair, they believe in what the Bible calls the thousand-year reign of Christ, but they just believe it to be a symbolic term and spiritual rather than natural in its understanding. This of course, is my own understanding of what they believe from my own study and interviews with those who hold to this viewpoint. They also believe that Christ is ruling and reigning right now from the Right Hand of The Father, and that His Kingdom has already come.

Problems With Amillennialism As I See It

For me this is a big problem. First, the Bible seems to indicate, pretty clearly I might add, that Christ will literally return to this planet, and literally set up His Kingdom for a one thousand-year timespan, which seems to be very literal. In Revelation 20 Verses 4-5 we read, ***"And I saw thrones, and they sat upon them, and*** *judgment was given unto them: and I saw the souls of them that were beheaded for the witness of Jesus, and for the word of God, and which had not worshipped the beast, neither his image, neither had received his mark upon their foreheads, or in their hands; <u>and they lived and reigned with Christ a thousand years</u>. But the rest of the dead lived not again until <u>the thousand years were finished</u>. This is the first resurrection."*

According to this viewpoint Jesus Christ's Kingdom is now. But, I see many passages in Scripture that point to a future Kingdom. One of those verses that stand out is in Zechariah 14 Verse 9 where it reads, *"And the LORD will be king over all the earth; in that day the LORD will be the only one, and His name the only one."*

Does that sound like the world today?

Another Issue

The other problem I see with this viewpoint is that because they believe Jesus began ruling at His ascension that also means Satan would have had to be bound at the same time. After all, the Bible says in Revelation 20 Verses 2-3 that Satan will be also bound for a *"thousand years"*. It states, *"And he laid hold <u>on the dragon, that old serpent, which is the Devil, and Satan, and bound him a thousand</u>*

years, And cast him into the bottomless pit, and shut him up, and set a seal upon him, that he should deceive the nations no more, till the thousand years should be fulfilled: and after that he must be loosed a little season."

So, if that timespan is a figurative thousand years and Jesus is ruling and reigning now, and Satan is bound, I would just like to ask, "How did he escape?"

I mean look at the world around us. I don't think for a second that Satan is bound, and if Amillennialism teaches the thousand years is figurative when concerning Jesus, they must then also use the same understanding about Satan. Just let me say, in my opinion, there is no way this could be true.

Postmillennial Lens

The second main viewpoint within Christianity is that of "Postmillennial". And, even though there are some who have overlap and theological lines have been blurred over the centuries, those in this camp believe the Millennium, as described in Scripture, is a time of great prosperity for Christ's Kingdom leading up to His return. Most believe that it will be a glorious time for the Church when they help to prepare and change the world into some kind of eutopia fit for Christ's return. They often believe that the Church will take over governments, the arts, media, etc. and turn this world into a glorious offering. They also don't necessarily believe in a thousand literal years, although some I spoke to do, but they mostly believe it to be a symbolic time-period in which the Church of Jesus Christ will have unparalleled success and revival. They often believe that prior to Christ's Second Coming the whole earth will be filled with the new Messianic Kingdom. It must be noted that the Postmillennial view was growing quite well until the first and second world wars and the re-birth of Israel as a nation. These factors seemed to quench the movement, but it has seen a resurgence in recent years.

Problems With Postmillennialism As I See It

The biggest problem I have with this view is that there is no way you can justify it with Scripture. There are too many Scriptures that point to horrible times just before the return of Jesus to this planet. Jesus Himself said it would be the worst time the world had ever seen (Matt 24). Even the verses used to point out the problems in Amillennialism debunk Postmillennialism. Revelation 20:4 once again, *"And I saw thrones, and they sat upon them, and judgment was given unto them: <u>and I saw the souls of</u>*

them that were beheaded for the witness of Jesus, and for the word of God, and which had not worshipped the beast, neither his image, neither had received his mark upon their foreheads, or in their hands; and they lived and reigned with Christ a thousand years. But the rest of the dead lived not again until the thousand years were finished. This is the first resurrection."

Here we see that these were "saints" or believers who lived during the last days Tribulation and they were beheaded for their witness of Jesus Christ.

What about 2 Timothy Chapter 3, the whole chapter? In verses 1-6 alone we read about the day just before Jesus returns, *"This know also, that in the last days perilous times shall come. For men shall be lovers of their own selves, covetous, boasters, proud, blasphemers, disobedient to parents, unthankful, unholy, Without natural affection, trucebreakers, false accusers, incontinent, fierce, despisers of those that are good, Traitors, heady, highminded, lovers of pleasures more than lovers of God; Having a form of godliness, but denying the power thereof: from such turn away. For of this sort are they which creep into houses, and lead captive silly women laden with sins, led away with divers lusts."*

Again, it's just my opinion, but there are so many passages that I believe debunk this theory. Nowhere in Scripture do I find passages that refer to the world getting better before the Return of Christ. I challenge you to study this out more.

Two Kinds of a Premillennial Lenses

The last main category of interpretation is "Premillennial", and it's the viewpoint I personally hold to. But, among this group there are two main categories. First, there are those who hold to a "classic" viewpoint which doesn't hold to a rapture theory and sometimes replaces Israel and its promises with the Church. This last idea about Israel can of course be found sometimes within both lenses previously mentioned, however, this classical approach does teach that there will be a revival among the Jewish people just before the return of Jesus.

My Lens: Premillennialism

The viewpoint I hold to is known as "Premillennialism". Without giving you an entire chapter on this I will simply say that this viewpoint believes that Jesus will remove His Church prior to the Millennium. It

The Quickly Approaching Rapture

also holds to the fact that in the Abrahamic covenant God gave the land of Israel to the Jews and He is not done with the Jewish people or the Land. This viewpoint believes that once the Church is removed in the Rapture, God will continue His work with Israel. However, it must be noted that this work will be accomplished through the Gospel of Jesus Christ. This group believes in a literal interpretation of Scripture unless clearly symbolic and that God will literally fulfill all the promises He made to Israel, and that Jesus will return at the end of the Tribulation and set up His Kingdom for one-thousand literal years. This means He will be ruling and reigning from Jerusalem while Satan is bound for that same timespan. At the end of the Millennium Satan will be released, tempt those alive on the Earth, Jesus will defeat all who come against Him, throw Satan into the Lake of Fire, and then burn up this universe and create a brand new Heaven and Earth where those who were saved by faith in Jesus Christ will live with Him forever! Okay, I gave you bonus material, but hey, it's my book.

    I hope you aren't lost so far but understanding these main lenses of interpretation should also help you understand the following four basic views of the Rapture within the Protestant/Evangelical community. There are of course others, but these are the main four.

Post-Tribulation Rapture Theory

First, we have what is called "Post-Tribulation" and those who hold to this view believe the Rapture of the Church of Jesus Christ will happen at the end of the time known as the Tribulation. We will dive into the definition and description of the "Tribulation" and the "Great Tribulation" in the next chapter. However, for the sake of this chapter just know the Tribulation is the terrible time-period on Earth leading up to the return of Jesus Christ. Those who hold to this theory of the Rapture believe that Jesus will come for His Church after this event called "The Great Tribulation." They do not believe that there will be a separation of the Church and Israel for seven appointed years. Some do believe that the Church and Israel will have to endure those seven years together. There are also some in the camp of "Post-Tribulation" that do, in fact, believe God is done with Israel. Again, not all, but some, and they believe that all the passages referring to Israel, or at least future passages, apply to the Church and not the nation or people of Israel.

The Quickly Approaching Rapture

Mid-Tribulation Rapture Theory

The next rapture theory to define is what's called the "Mid-Tribulation" theory. This is exactly what it sounds like. Those who hold to this theory believe that Jesus will take His people out of the Great Tribulation at the middle point of the event. This corresponds with what the Bible seems to indicate as "The Abomination of Desolation" (Mat 24:15, Dan.9:27). This is the time in which the Anti-Christ will go into the newly established Jewish Temple in Jerusalem and defile it, proclaim that he is god, and the Jewish people will reject him. At this point the Anti-Christ will turn against the Jewish people and seek to kill them (Mat 24:16-21). However, God will preserve a faithful remnant of Jewish believers in Christ for the last three-and-a-half years of the Tribulation.

It is at this middle point, the "Abomination of Desolation", that the Mid-Tribulation Rapture Theory believes that Christians will be removed. Those who hold to this theory do so primarily because they believe that there are significant passages in Scripture that proclaim Christians will not have to endure the wrath of God because it was satisfied in Christ. They further believe that the Wrath of God will only be poured out in the second half of the "Tribulation". This last half is what is commonly referred to as "The Great Tribulation".

Pre-Wrath Rapture Theory

This Mid-Tribulation understanding is similar to another theory which is called "The Pre-Wrath" theory. This is the theory that believes essentially that the Church will be raptured out before the Wrath of God is poured out on earth. They do not define a clear timeline for that, but most indicate around ¾ of the way through the Tribulation.

Special or Selective Rapture

While this next mention is not one of the main four categories of Rapture theories, I feel I must explain that there are some in the Church who believe the Rapture will only be for special or selective Christians. They believe, or seem to believe, that they are one of these special Christians, and that they are defined as the "really good Christians". In other words, the Rapture will only happen for a select few Christians who are overcomers and living right. There are also those who call this a "partial rapture".

While I don't hold to this view, I do believe that some who call themselves Christians will be left behind. I think that the Rapture is "special" in that, only those who are born again and have the Spirit of God living in them

The Quickly Approaching Rapture

will be taken. But I also believe many who call themselves "Christians" will be left behind because they were never really born again (See Matthew 7). However, the special, limited, partial or selective rapture folks seem to believe true Christians who aren't living right will be left behind. I don't personally hold to that.

Pre-Tribulation Rapture Theory

The final theory that this book will mention is the one that I defend as the most viable. This theory is what is known as the "Pre-Tribulation Rapture Theory". The understanding among those who hold to a "Pre-Tribulation" theory is that Jesus Christ will remove His Church prior to the entire Tribulation period. This is done for three main reasons according to the theory. First, to remove the Church from the earth so that His wrath can be poured out on the world that has rejected the free offer of salvation through Christ and have refused to repent of their sins. Second, this is done before the tribulation to allow God to deal with the nation of Israel corporately for a period of seven years as prophesied in Daniel Chapter 9. This time-period is known as the "Seventieth Week of Daniel" or, "Time of Jacob's Trouble", and it will be God bringing the nation of Israel to a place of acceptance of His Son Jesus Christ.

Third, while there are probably many other reasons for the pre-tribulation timing, the last one mentioned for the sake of this book is the what is called "The Marriage Supper of the Lamb". This can be compared to a honeymoon with the Lord and His Church, also often called "His Bride" among Christians, for a seven-year period in Heaven. This is the same place that those holding to this theory believe is being described by Jesus in John 14:3. Jesus said, *"And if I go and prepare a place for you, I will come again, and receive you unto myself; that where I am, there ye may be also."*

Those who believe in the Pre-Tribulation Rapture also believe that the "place" Jesus is talking about is where the Church will remain during the duration of the Seventieth Week of Daniel, Tribulation, and Great Tribulation.

Five Views of Eschatology

The final section of this chapter will briefly share with you the five main view of eschatology (This simply is the study of last things or end times) within the Christian Church. These are also lenses, but they are specifically how each group interprets end times events in general. These are simply how various Christians within the three lenses of Amillennial, Postmillennial and Premillennial view end times events. There is no way to cleanly arrange how this is done. It really seems like many just mix and match.

Preterism

Preterists and partial Preterists believe that the events written about concerning the Tribulation have already occurred or have mostly occurred. Most Preterists I have talked to also hold to the belief that God has continued His promises to Israel through the Church.

Futurism

The Futurist look at the events in Revelation and other prophetic books of the Bible as future events.

Historicism

Those in the Historical camp usually apply prophetic passages to people and events. They often apply biblical symbols and imagery to world leaders, etc.

Idealism

Those in this camp often use an allegorical or symbolic approach to prophetic passages. Often they hold to a nonliteral approach to Scripture as a whole. Some interpret the signs and symbols from a spiritual aspect rather than a Scriptural basis.

Dispensationalism

I am one in the camp of Dispensationalism. However, I am also careful to understand that this is a system recognized by man. It is not something named in Scripture. This is a way to organize and understand how God has worked with man on Earth since the creation. Some divide it in different ways, but for the context of this study just know that most dispensationalists believe God has done just that. We believe that God has utilized different "Dispensations" which are really just periods of time in which He administered with the world and His people in different ways. In other words, God used different ages in dealing with man. These are often separated into seven "ages" or "Dispensations". The most common understandings are "Innocents" the time in the Garden of Eden with Adam and Eve before the fall of man. This was followed by "Conscience" during the pre-flood era. After the flood it was "Human Government" which was started with the basis of all human law in Genesis 9:6 and the establishment of the death penalty for murder. After this it is often noted that from Abraham's time until Moses it was the time of "Promise". Then from Moses to Jesus it was the time of the "Law". At the Cross Jesus established the time of "Grace" and the last dispensation will be the "Millennial Kingdom" a one-thousand-year reign of Christ on planet Earth.

Those who hold to this theory are all about a literal interpretation of Scripture and that there is a distinction between what God is doing with the Church and with Israel. However, we certainly don't believe that there is salvation outside of Christ. Most dispensationalists that I know believe that many within Israel will turn to Jesus during the Tribulation, and that the time of the Tribulation is partially to fulfill God's promise to them, and to complete the 490 years allotted to them in Daniel 9. This is why the seven-year period of Tribulation is also called "The Time of Jacob's Trouble."

Chapter 4

The Time of Jacob's Trouble

The Tribulation Vs. The Great Tribulation

As mentioned, the Mid-Tribulation and Pre-Wrath theories teach that the Church will have to endure some of the Tribulation. But, in the case of Post-Tribulation theorists they believe the Church will go through the entire thing, including what is called "The Great Tribulation". For the sake of a proper understanding for this entire book it is necessary to pause here and define the biblical term "Tribulation" and what is known as "The Great Tribulation."

The "Tribulation" is commonly known as the entire last days' time-period leading up to Christ's return. This is most understood to be seven years in length. However, "The Great Tribulation" is often defined as the time within the Tribulation in which God's pours out His wrath on the world. There is disagreement in the various camps as to when this exactly starts. As previously mentioned the Mid-

The Quickly Approaching Rapture

Trib folks think it starts at the mid-point (3 ½ years) the Pre-Wrath say it's about ¾ the way through.

Pre-Tribulation Rapture adherents, like myself, believe that God will pour out His increasing wrath starting near, or at the beginning of the Tribulation, and the entire seven-years is a time when God has promised His Bride a honeymoon with Him in a place He has prepared. They also generally believe that the entire seven-years is a time when God will once again deal with Israel corporately.

This Already Happened?

When looking at the various theories of the Rapture, as previously mentioned, some in the Christian Church, namely preterists, who believe this "Great Tribulation" has already occurred. Again, they believe that all or some of these events happened with the destruction of Jerusalem in 70 A.D. and that it doesn't point to any future events, or many of the events named by Jesus Himself. However, two very glaring issues hinder this theory. First, in the book of Matthew Chapter 24 verse 21 Jesus is speaking to His disciples about this time of tribulation which is coming upon the whole earth. Jesus says, *"For then shall be great tribulation, such as was not since the beginning of the world to this time, no, nor ever shall be."* In this passage

The Quickly Approaching Rapture

Jesus clearly states that the time of tribulation He is speaking of is going to be far worse than anything the world has ever seen, and it will be so bad that nothing else will ever be worse than it.

In analyzing this passage, it seems obvious that the destruction of Jerusalem and the Temple cannot be the events described by Jesus. It may be argued that many nations have endured far worse over the centuries. World War II saw the detonation of nuclear weapons on Japanese cities, six million Jews were killed in the Holocaust, and what about multiple leaders in history and their murderous administrations. Men like Stalin, Mao, Caligula, Attila the Hun, Tomas de Torquemada, Ivan the Terrible, Mussolini, Pol Pot and Hitler himself. They all did unspeakable atrocities that can be classified as worse than that which occurred in 70 A.D. Not only that, but the time described in the book of Revelation known as the "Great Tribulation" says that in just one of the horrible events described that a third of the world's population will be killed (Rev. 9:14-15). Even if you subtract a good number of people because of the Rapture, it could still be as many as 2-3 billion people killed in this single event during the Great Tribulation. Also, in Jesus' statement He states that whatever is coming is worse than anything that has ever happened before in the world's history. Let's think about that. Whatever is coming was worse than the flood of Noah's day, which was prior to what Jesus is describing. Not to take anything away from the pain and suffering of 70 A.D., but in context, the events being described by Jesus seem far worse than the thousands dying in Jerusalem during that time.

Also, the very fact that Israel is a nation again after being birthed in a single day on May 14, 1948 (Isa. 66:8), seems to disprove the theory that 70 A.D. was the time of tribulation. The Book of Daniel goes on to explain that there will be an additional seven years in which God will deal corporately with the Jewish nation and its people. This time period is what the Bible calls "The Time of Jacob's Trouble." If the nation had not been reborn, which the Bible prophesied would happen, how then would this be accomplished? The answer is—it couldn't have.

Seventy Weeks of Years

This is another key point for this book. The "Time of Jacob's Trouble" must be addressed. It comes from a passage in Daniel Chapter 9 verse 24 which states, ***"Seventy weeks are determined upon thy people*** *and upon thy holy city, to finish the transgression, and to make an end of sins, and to make reconciliation for iniquity, and to bring in everlasting righteousness, and to seal up the vision and prophecy, and to anoint the most Holy."*

This is very important because this passage indicates that *"seventy weeks"* which can be further understood from verse 25 as being 70 weeks of years, or 490 total years are *"determined"* for Israel. Daniel 9:25 reads, *"Know therefore and understand, that from the going forth of the commandment to restore and to build Jerusalem unto the Messiah the Prince shall be <u>seven weeks, and threescore and two weeks</u>: the street shall be built again, and the wall, even in troublous times."*

To break this down in a way we can understand the Bible is saying that 490 literal years have been assigned to Israel. It also says that *"seven weeks, and threescore and two weeks"* which is literally 483 total years would occur from the time the decree to rebuild Jerusalem until the Messiah would come. Just so you know, this happened exactly.

I have to make a correction from an earlier publication. It seems I picked the wrong decree when discussing this

The Quickly Approaching Rapture

topic. We know from Scripture there are three commands pertaining to the rebuilding of Jerusalem. There is one from Cyrus one from Darius but the one that fits this prophecy best is found in Nehemiah Chapter 2. This is when Artaxerxes makes a decree on March 14, 445 B.C. It then took 49 years to get Jerusalem up and running which accounts for the first **"seven weeks"** that Daniel 9:25 states. Then, from that point there are another **"threescore and two weeks"** or sixty-two weeks of years which is a total of 483 years which lines up perfectly with the time of Jesus Christ. In fact, if you can't the exact number of days from the decree of Artaxerxes you land on Palm Sunday in 32 A.D., which is the exact day Jesus rode into Jerusalem on a colt of a donkey.

God tells us in Daniel 9 that 490 years would be set aside for Israel, but that from the time the command is given to rebuild Jerusalem until *"Messiah the Prince"* would be 483 literal years. Then, verse 25 of Daniel 9 says that at that same time-period Messiah would be *"cut off"*. Which is quite a remarkable prophecy pointing to the crucifixion of Christ. It reads, *"*"Know therefore and understand, that from the going forth of the commandment to restore and to build Jerusalem unto the*

The Quickly Approaching Rapture

Messiah the Prince shall be seven weeks, and threescore and two weeks: the street shall be built again, and the wall, even in troublous times. And after threescore and two weeks <u>shall Messiah be cut off,</u> but not for himself:"

In a nutshell, God issued 490 total years concerning Israel. He did so to, *"finish the transgression, and to make an end of sins, and to make reconciliation for iniquity, and to bring in everlasting righteousness."*

However, those 490 years were interputed after 483 with Christ's first coming. This means there are seven more literal years assigned to Israel.

But, if we read Romans Chapter 11 we know why this delay was allowed by God. Verses 25-27 in Romans 11 are some of the most important in the Scriptures concerning the Church and Israel, *"For I would not, brethren, that ye should be ignorant of this mystery, lest ye should be wise in your own conceits; <u>that blindness in part is happened to Israel, until the fulness of the Gentiles be come in.</u> And so, all Israel shall be saved: as it is written, There shall come out of Sion the Deliverer, and shall turn away ungodliness from Jacob: For this is my covenant unto them, when I shall take away their sins."*

Look at this passage again. First, God explains that Israel was blinded (in part) for a season. I believe that began at the 483-year mark, or when Messiah was *"cut off"*. It then explains that this will continue until the *"fullness of the Gentiles be come in"*. I believe the fullness it speaks of is completed at the Rapture. Also, this passage states that *"all Israel shall be saved"* and the *"Deliverer"* will *"turn away ungodliness from Jacob"* (Israel).

Remember the passage in Daniel 9 states that the seventy weeks assigned to Israel were *"to <u>finish the transgression</u>, and to <u>make an end of sins</u>, and to make <u>reconciliation for iniquity</u>, and to <u>bring in everlasting righteousness</u>."*

This seems to line up perfectly with what is being said in Romans 11. Looking at it all we see that 490 literal years were assigned to Israel, 483 of those years were completed with Christ and with the partial blinding of Israel. This will continue until the *"fullness of the Gentiles come in"* and at that point seven more literal years will be determined for Israel to complete God's plan and bring them into His Kingdom!

Chapter 5

God's Wrath

The Day of the Lord

Often times when I hear people speaking about the "Day of the Lord" they do so as a single day when Christ returns to Earth. But, that isn't exactly what the Bible is saying. In Joel 2 verse 1 it is written, ***"Blow ye the trumpet in Zion, and sound an alarm in my holy mountain: let all the inhabitants of the land tremble: for <u>the day of the Lord</u> cometh, for it is nigh at hand."*** Pastor Jon Courson writes in his *Application Commentary of the New Testament*, "Joel 2 speaks about the Day of the Lord, the day when the church is raptured and judgment comes down."[v] In other words, we know that during what the Bible declares "The Day of the Lord" many different events will happen. It's a span of time and not a single day.

We will see soon in this Chapter that the very first set of plagues describes this fact. The "Day of the Lord" is best understood as the troubling time just before the return of Jesus. This is most likely the entire seven-year

Tribulation, and it's the period of time when God pours out His wrath on this world.

Very Troubling Times

God's wrath is something that no one wants to experience. The non-believer will experience it at some point if they do not receive the free gift of salvation. That wrath will come in the form of judgment and eternal separation from God in a real place called Hell. However, before that happens we read in Revelation Chapter 6 that God is going to pour out His wrath on this world, and upon those alive during what is known as "The Great Tribulation" or "Time of Jacob's Trouble."

In the very first set of plagues in the Tribulation, Revelation 6 explains that an event will occur when every person on the planet scatters because of what has come upon the Earth. But note, the people seem to understand that the events transpiring are the wrath of God, and these two verses found in Revelation 6:16-17 explain just that, ***"And said to the mountains and rocks, Fall on us, and hide us from the face of him that sitteth on the throne, and from <u>the wrath of the Lamb</u>: For <u>the great day of his wrath is come</u>; and who shall be able to stand?"***

The Quickly Approaching Rapture

Christians Won't Endure God's Wrath

The wrath of God being poured out during the Tribulation is one of the reasons those who believe in a Pre-Tribulation Rapture do so. The Bible declares in 1 Thessalonians 5:9, *"For God **hath not appointed us** to wrath, but to obtain salvation by our Lord Jesus Christ."* If Christians are not appointed to God's wrath, the pre-tribulationist would argue, then the Church will not have to endure the tribulation. After all, in the first set of plagues listed in Chapter 6 it is clear that God is pouring out His wrath on the world and its inhabitants. This means the Mid-Tribulation theory, the Pre-Wrath theory and certainly the Post-Tribulation theory all disagree. Because, we see God's wrath being poured out in the very first set of plagues of Revelation.

The late Pastor Chuck Smith, in his book *What the World is Coming To,* agreed. He wrote, "The very fact that "the great day" is the day of God's wrath, "the wrath of the Lamb," would again preclude the church being upon the earth. "For God has not appointed us to wrath" (I Thessalonians 5:9)."[vi] Pastor Chuck went on to point out an example of this truth from the story in Genesis 18 concerning the destruction of Sodom and Gomorrah. We know that Abraham asked God to spare the cities if there were but fifty righteous living in them. Genesis 18:26 states, **"And the LORD said, If I find in Sodom fifty righteous within the city, then I will spare all the place for their sakes."** Seeing his opening Abraham then proceeded to lower the number. What about 45?, 40?, 30?, 20?, and finally asks the Lord in verse 32 that if just 10 be found righteous would He spare them? God said He would. However, we know from the rest of the story that ten righteous were not found. We also know that just before the destruction of the cities God sent His angels to remove Lot and his family, although Lot's wife didn't make it. She was caught looking back, which actually proved where her heart was. Pastor Chuck explains 2 Peter 2:9 is in response to this rescue of God's people.[vii] It states, **"The Lord knoweth how to deliver the godly out of temptations, and to reserve the unjust unto the day of judgment to be punished."**

When you look at the Scriptures there are examples like the one we see in the story of Lot. One might argue that no bigger example can be found than that of the flood. If you look at the story of Noah, he and his family were saved from destruction. God instructed Noah to build an Ark, get the provisions on board, and then God Himself sealed the Ark to protect Noah and his family and bring them out of the devastation. In Genesis 7 verse 16 we read, ***"And they that went in, went in male and female of all flesh, as God had commanded him: and the <u>LORD shut him in</u>."*** This is significant because it was by God's command and action that Noah and his family were saved. In verse 17 it states that as the waters increased Noah and his family were lifted ***"up above the earth."*** In the same way Lot and his family were taken out of Sodom by angels just before its destruction, Noah was sealed by God and lifted up above the earth during the deluge. For born again Christians, who are sealed, they too will be lifted up to be with the Lord just before the greatest tribulation the world has ever known. Matthew 24 verse 37 reads, ***"But as the days of Noah were, so shall also the coming of the Son of man be."*** Verse 38 explains, ***"For as in the days that were before the flood they were eating and drinking, marrying and giving in marriage, until the day that Noah entered into the ark."*** Verse 39 concludes, ***"And knew not until the flood came, and took them all away; <u>so, shall also the coming of the Son of man be</u>."***

The Quickly Approaching Rapture

The book of Luke Chapter 17 uses this same example of Noah but it also includes the story of Lot. Luke compares the coming of Jesus with both. In verse 28-30 it is written, *"Likewise also <u>as it was in the days of Lot</u>; they did eat, they drank, they bought, they sold, they planted, they builded; But the same day that Lot went out of Sodom it rained fire and brimstone from heaven, and destroyed them all. <u>Even thus shall it be in the day when the Son of man is revealed.</u>"*

You Can't Fake it or You Won't Make It!

In this same Chapter of Luke there is a warning for those who fake it. God's wrath is a serious thing, and I wonder how many Christians are simply a Christian by name only? I wonder how many, like lot's wife, are really in love with this world and the stuff of this world and not in love with Jesus? Luke 17:32 states, *"Remember Lot's wife."* It goes on in verse 33 to explain, *"Whosoever shall seek to save his life shall lose it; and whosoever shall lose his life shall preserve it."*

The Quickly Approaching Rapture

I beg you. Please, don't fake being a Christian. But, before I jump too far forward I must tell you that the real problem is some of you don't know you're faking it! Matthew 7 talks about those who prophesied, cast out demons, and did *"many wonderful works"* in the name of Jesus. But we know many of them will have to suffer the wrath of God! Matthew 7:25 is Jesus' reply to those who claim to have done all these things in His name. He says, ***"And then will I profess unto them, I never knew you: depart from me, ye that work iniquity."***

You know, I want to stop here and name drop. Do you know that I know the President? I know him. I know all about him. That's right I know the President.....

I mean, he doesn't know me. He doesn't even know my name or anything about me…. but I know him. I know of him. I know all about him.

See, it doesn't matter if you "know" Jesus. It doesn't even matter if you "know about" Jesus or His Word. The only thing that matters is if Jesus knows you.

Jesus is coming for His Church, and just like Noah and Lot He will have us removed just before destruction comes. The Tribulation will be a time when He pours out His wrath on this planet and everything alive on it. It will be worse than the flood, worse than Sodom and Gomorrah, and worse than anything we can imagine or think. Don't get left behind looking at the world like Lot's wife. Jesus wants a faithful wife not a cheating wife. He wants those who are born again, filled with His Spirit, living for Him and denying themselves.

If you are caught up in a man-centered gospel. If you are believing in a Christianity that teaches you experience or materialism over obedience. If you are living a Christian lie rather than a Christian life—Repent!

Too many so-called Christians are infatuated with this world. They are trying to build their own little kingdoms. Many are lifting themselves up, promoting themselves, it's all about them. Well, Jesus will explain to them He never knew them. You think you know Him, but He doesn't know you! This scares me so much for people I know and love. I have known, and know people, who call themselves believers but they are so caught up in this world. They say they are Christians but I just don't know. I pray for them. I pray for the churches they attend that teach worldly things. I pray that they will repent before it's too late. The problem is many don't think there is a problem. In fact, they think people like me are the problem. They call us things like legalists or mock our faith because we go through hard times, suffer, have sickness, and the like. They claim its sin in our lives or we just don't have enough faith to be healed, blessed, or whatever else they think is "good."

I believe God heals. I believe He blesses. I believe He still equips His Church with His Gifts through His Spirit. But, I also know that His people endure hardship. We suffer. We pick up our crosses daily and follow Him. I also know that if the world hated Him they will hate us. Yet, so many, so-called churches, are embraced by many in the world, or they are attempting to out world the world.

I am not saying this to argue, fight, or anything else that might question my motives. People, Jesus is coming! He is coming for His Bride. He desires an obedient Church not one that does their own thing. I fear for those who will hear Jesus say to them, *"depart from me you worker of iniquity, I never knew you."*

The Quickly Approaching Rapture

Please, please, please, don't let that be you or anyone you know. God's wrath is coming upon this world. It will be poured out on those who have rejected His son, even if they don't realize they have done this by their horrible theology, a false gospel and a world-based faith. However, His wrath will never be tasted by those who truly know Him, and more importantly, by those whom He truly knows. They will instead partake of the sweet taste of victory in the form of a wedding feast with their Lord.

Please, I beg you. Before it's too late.

Remember Lot's wife.

Chapter 6

Is The Rapture a New Doctrine?

Darby, Darby, Darby

Whenever I participate in a friendly debate or I am asked about the doctrine of the Rapture, inevitably someone brings up Darby. Many who reject the Rapture say that Pastor John Nelson Darby is the one who created this doctrine, that he made it up, and there is no biblical evidence for it. In fact, those who tend to argue this point with me usually express that there is no evidence of this doctrine prior to 1830, and that no Church or denomination taught it, nor was their any official statement on it, nor was it taught within any Churches catechisms. To which I usually say, "So what?"

Now before I go forward, I think it's important to state that I am not opposed to denominations nor am I opposed to creeds, statements of faith or denominational teachings. All of these things can have value of course. What I am saying is that I don't go to any of the aforementioned things for my doctrine and neither should

The Quickly Approaching Rapture

you. Also, one of the things I might suggest when it relates to the doctrine of the Rapture is that the teaching of this doctrine seems to be plainly written in the Bible. If people didn't teach on it much in the early Church, there could be a reason. Maybe God limited the understanding of such until the very end of Church history? Although, I don't believe this to be true, it could be suggested. Also, what if the doctrine has always been taught, but it was taught under a different name?

"Wait, what do you mean by that?" You ask.

"And I am so glad you did!"

What if the doctrine of the Rapture was taught as the imminent return of Jesus?

"The what?" You ask.

"The imminent return of Jesus Christ."

If you look at the word "Imminent" which means simply something that is about to happen or could happen at any moment, I suggest to you that this doctrine only makes sense if you believe in what some of us call the Rapture. The reason for this is two-fold. First, there are critical Scriptures that point to the time when Jesus will come back to this planet and set up His Kingdom. Just before that time we know there will be a time of great tribulation worse than anything the world has never seen before. And, yet, there are also passages that state that Jesus could come at any moment for His people.

So, which is it?

A bunch of events have to happen before Jesus comes back or He could come at any moment? I tell you both are true, and this can only be understood by the fact that Jesus comes first, <u>for</u> His Church and then returns, <u>with</u> His Church to set up His Kingdom. We will look at key passages in the next Chapter that support this understanding. But, just know, the Bible clearly teaches two events.

Early Church Examples

Going back to the early Church teaching of the Rapture. If what I believe is true, that the imminent return of Jesus is what the Rapture doctrine is built on, then it is clear, in my opinion, that this was taught in the early Church.

Didache

First, there is a document called the *Didache*. It is sometimes called *The Lord's Teaching Through the Twelve*, or similar. It usually is dated in the first century, but some estimates I have seen claim it could be early second century. Either way, it's early, and it was a document written to help those in the Church understand practices and teachings. Of course, that's the very simplistic definition, but I challenge you to go and read it yourself.

So, what does the *Didache* say about the Rapture? Well, nothing, or a lot, depending on what you mean by Rapture, and by what lens you see it through. If you mean that the Lord could come back at any moment then it clearly states that. In Chapter 16 the opening line states, "*Watch for your life's sake. Let not your lamps be quenched, nor your loins unloosed; but be ready, <u>for you know not the hour in which our Lord will come</u>.*"[viii]

The Quickly Approaching Rapture

The *Didache* goes on to explain that horrible times will come in the last days. It states, *"For in the last days false prophets and corrupters shall be multiplied, and the sheep shall be turned into wolves, and love shall be turned into hate; for when lawlessness increases, they shall hate and persecute and betray one another, and then shall appear the world-deceiver as Son of God, and shall do signs and wonders, and the earth shall be delivered into his hands, and he shall do iniquitous things which have never yet come to pass since the beginning."*[ix] It then has something interesting to say to believers. It first acknowledges that a *"fire of trial"* will come, *"and many shall be made to stumble and shall perish."*[x] However, it then states, *"But those who endure in their faith <u>shall be saved from under the curse itself</u>."* But, just how will they be saved? The *Didache* then states, *"And then shall appear the signs of the truth: first, the sign of an outspreading in heaven, then the sign of the sound of the trumpet. And third, the resurrection of the dead -- yet not of all, but as it is said: "The Lord shall come and all His saints with Him."* The last line in the *Didache* then says, *"Then shall the world see the Lord coming upon the clouds of heaven."*

The Quickly Approaching Rapture

So, here we see an outline of end times events according to those in the early Church. We have already found out that they believed Jesus could come at any moment and so they were called to live godly. We also know that they believed times would become evil in the last days, and that fake Christians would be revealed as wolves and that the love of many would grow cold. The document then states that a fake messiah, a fake "Son of God" would come on the scene, and that this evil man, which we know will be the Anti-Christ, *"shall do signs and wonders, and the earth shall be delivered into his hands, and he shall do iniquitous things which have never yet come to pass since the beginning."*

I pause here to pose a question.

"So, Which is it?"

"Huh?" You ask.

"Well, is it that the Lord can come at any moment for His people or will they have to wait around for the Anti-Christ?"

"I don't get what you're asking," You might say.

"Well, simply this...."

The Quickly Approaching Rapture

We read, *"be ready, for you know not the hour in which our Lord will come."* This is a statement from the *Didache*, and yet, the same author is saying that there will be terrible times *"in the last days"*.

"So what?" You ask.

This is clearly stating that the author believes that the Christians don't have to wait for anything to happen before Christ comes back for them. He tells them to be ready because they don't know the time and then he also teaches that in the last days horrible times will come and the Ant-Christ will be revealed. He is clearly teaching one before the other. In essence, nothing has to happen before Jesus comes for us so be ready, but after we are gone, there are going to be horrible times including this man of sin the Anti-Christ.

It simply can't be both without two different events!

Also, look at what the *Didache* is saying about those horrible times. It clearly states that a, *"fire of trial"* will come, *"and many shall be made to stumble and shall perish."* It then states, *"But those who endure in their faith shall be saved from under the curse itself."*

"Do you see it?"

"No, and you are repeating yourself," you say.

"I know! I feel I must, and don't worry we aren't done yet!"

It is saying that those who endure **in their faith**, not in the tribulation or endure the trial of fire, but they endure **in their faith**, it's those who will be saved **from under the curse**. This lines up with a passage in Revelation 3 verse 10 when Jesus gives a promise to His faithful Church, *"Because thou hast kept the word of my patience, I also will keep thee from the hour of temptation, which shall come upon all the world, to try them that dwell upon the earth."*

We will look closer at this in a future Chapter when we look at the Seven Letters to the Seven Churches, but needless to say, there is a clear similarity with the verse in Revelation and the sentence in Chapter 16 of the *Didache*.

When looking at Chapter 16 of the *Didache* as an outline it seems to bring things together. First, the faithful Church needs to be ready because Jesus could come at any moment. Second, there is coming evil times in which many false prophets and fake Christians will arise. Love will turn into lawlessness, and the Anti-Christ will appear. Third, this time will become a time of "fire of trial". Fourth, those who endure <u>in their faith,</u> just like it is stated in the first sentence of chapter 16, "<u>shall be saved from under the curse itself</u>".

We then see an overall outline of events in the last section calling them "the signs of truth". First, "an outspreading of Heaven" and then "the sign of the sound of the trumpet" and then "the resurrection of the dead" and "the Lord shall come and all His saints with Him." Which, that last statement is similar to the passage in 1 Thessalonians 3:13 where it states, *"To the end he may stablish your hearts unblameable in holiness before God, even our Father, at the coming of our Lord Jesus Christ with all his saints."* I also believe the overall alignment of this section can be further understood by 1 Thessalonians Chapter 4 verses 16 and 17, *"For the Lord himself shall descend from heaven with a shout, with the voice of the archangel, and with the trump of God: and the dead in Christ shall rise first: Then we which are alive and remain shall be caught up together with them in the*

The Quickly Approaching Rapture

clouds, to meet the Lord in the air: and so shall we ever be with the Lord."

In Verse 18 of this same Chapter then states, *"Wherefore comfort one another with these words."*

In my opinion, It wouldn't be very comforting if the author is telling the Church that they will have to go through the trial of fire coming upon the whole earth known as the Tribulation. The time in which God Himself will pour out His wrath on the world and all that are in it. No! Instead, the author, under the inspiration of the Holy Spirit is saying that the Lord is coming to get them before it all takes place. We are going to look at this passage more in a future Chapter so I will stop here for now.

Another However

I also want to say that I have seen the same document I just quoted as evidence that the early Church didn't teach about the imminent return of Jesus. I have seen scholars who have a different lenses come to opposite conclusions. This is why I included the section on the lenses because the lens you view Scripture and/or

The Quickly Approaching Rapture

eschatology through, will determine how you see topics like this. I could do the same with some of the early Church Father's and their teachings. While I see it as teaching that Christ could come at any moment someone with a differing lens will say that they see it as events must still happen before Christ's return for His Church.

It must also be noted that there was a good amount of teaching in the early Church that isn't exactly lined up with Scripture so any use of it can be negated by those who choose to. Remember, just because something was written early doesn't make it right. In fact, the early Church spent a lot of time fighting heresy and false teaching. We see this evidenced even in the Bible itself through the writings of Paul the Apostle.

This is why using the Bible as our source for any doctrine is very important. I am only using early sources to answer the critics in relation to what they claim about the Rapture being a doctrine created in the nineteenth century. My hope is to show you the imminent return of Jesus seems to have been clearly taught in the early Church, and I believe it is clearly taught in the Bible as well.

The Quickly Approaching Rapture

More Evidence

While it must be admitted that evidence of a clear teaching of the Rapture is somewhat rare within early Church history, it must also be admitted that many of the early Church teachings had an element of teaching relating to Christ coming at any moment. This teaching, as noted, can be understood as the imminent return of Christ. However, there are some examples of early teaching of the Rapture in a way that those who claim it was an invention of the nineteenth century and John Nelson Darby just don't like to see. In fact, after giving a few examples to some of those critics I have witnessed a very unloving amount of animosity and quick dismissal. I have seen many try to argue these following examples away, but in the end, I have seen nothing that is convincing that these aren't teaching about a Pre-Tribulation Rapture.

Ephraem the Syrian

In an early Church sermon attributed to Ephraem the Syrian (4th Century), there seems to be a reference to the Rapture of the Church in his work known at the "Apocalypse of Pseudo-Ephraem". Don Stewart in His book *The Rapture An Introduction to the Blessed Hope of*

The Quickly Approaching Rapture

the Church quotes this sermon translation. It states, *"All the saints and elect of God are gathered together before the tribulation, which is to come, and are taken to the Lord, in order that they may not see at any time the confusion which overwhelms the world because of our sins."*[xi]

While some discount this and claim it was written as late as the eighth century, or that somehow this wasn't what he was speaking of, the fact remains that a few different translations seem to agree on the meaning. And, whether penned in the fourth or eight centuries, it is still much earlier than John Darby in the nineteenth century.

The Shepherd of Hermas

There is a late first century or perhaps an early second century document which covers end times events called the *Shepherd of Hermas*. From my own study I have found that this was a popular document during the early Church, and some even considered it canonical. However, I am certainly not holding it to that level. The author of the writing is a man named Hermas. Most believe him to be a Roman believer, and some even suggest it is the same "Hermas" Paul greets in Romans 16:14. Note that some translations spell it Hermas and some Hermes. *Strong's*

The Quickly Approaching Rapture

spells it Hermas (G2057). In any case, this man Hermas was a Christian in Rome and his writing was embraced by many in the early Church. For the sake of this book I want to point out some curious things that he wrote. To do that I think it's important to give you an overview of how the book is organized. It's divided in three sections. First, the Visions, which contains five such visions. Second, the Commandments which has twelve commandment writings. Lastly, the Similitudes which has a total of ten.

In the first section and Vision 4 the author starts out by writing about a vision relating to a time of coming "Tribulation". As his vision progresses, he sees a few notable things. He sees what he calls a *"virgin arrayed as if she were going forth from a bridal-chamber all in white."*[xii] He then notes that he knows this virgin represents the Church. He goes on to explain his experience to this woman about a beast he had encountered, but that he had escaped. The virgin tells him, *"Thou hast escaped a great tribulation by reason of thy faith."*[xiii] At that point the most powerful statement is then uttered by this woman, *"Go therefore, and declare to the elect of the Lord His mighty works, and tell them that <u>this beast is a type of the great</u>*

The Quickly Approaching Rapture

<u>tribulation which is to come</u>. If therefore ye prepare yourselves beforehand, and repent (and turn) unto the Lord with your whole heart, <u>ye shall be able to escape it</u>, if your heart be made pure and without blemish, and if for the remaining days of your life ye serve the Lord blamelessly."[xiv]

I think this is a pretty clear example of early church writings about the Rapture. Sure, it doesn't say how we will escape the Tribulation, but there is certainly the understanding that escape will come to the faithful.

Victorinus: Commentary on the Apocalypse

Another early Church example of the teaching of the Rapture can be found in the works of Victorinus of Pettau. This man wrote nine commentaries. The one we will be looking at is his commentary on "The Apocalypse", also known as Revelation. It is dated in the late third and maybe early fourth century. From his commentary chapter 15 verse 1 it states, *"And I saw another great and wonderful sign, seven angels having the seven last plagues; for in them is completed the indignation of God."- For the wrath of God always strikes the obstinate people with seven plagues, that is, perfectly, as it is said in Leviticus; and*

The Quickly Approaching Rapture

these shall be <u>in the last time</u>, when the <u>Church shall have gone out of the midst</u>."[xv] In Chapter 6 he also eludes to this same thing. He writes, *"And the heaven withdrew as a scroll that is rolled up." For the heaven to be rolled away, that is, that <u>the Church shall be taken away</u>."*[xvi]

The bottom line is that some in the early Church did teach that the Church would escape or be removed before the Tribulation. Also, it must be noted once again that just because it was scarce, and that the doctrine seems to have taken centuries to unfold, it really shouldn't be surprising. Many key Church doctrines took hundreds of years to be solidified within the Church. I don't understand completely why this is the case with any of those doctrines, but in the case of the Rapture I can see why God would allow it not to grow in its understanding until the end of the age.

Chapter 7

The Imminent Return of Jesus Christ

Scriptural Evidence

I have already explained what the word "imminent" means. It simply means "something that is about to happen or could happen at any moment." While I presented a few early Church examples, mostly just to prove that this is not a brand-new doctrine made up by John Darby, I think going to Scripture for our own study is needed. In this chapter I am going to present to you a few passages in the Bible that point to the fact that Jesus could come at any moment for His Church. I believe the evidence is obvious.

Two Stages

When searching the Scriptures, we see that Jesus had a lot to say about the Rapture. First, He made a promise. In John 14:1-3 Jesus says, *"Let not your heart be troubled: ye believe in God, believe also in me. In my Father's house are many mansions: if it were not so, I would have told you. <u>I go to prepare a place for you.</u> And if I go and prepare a place for you, <u>I will come again, and</u>*

receive you unto myself; that where I am, there ye may be also."

Notice, Jesus says He is going to prepare a place for His Church. Second, He says He will *"come again"* and *"receive you unto myself."* This is key because the passage that tells us about the Rapture itself in 1 Thessalonians states that Jesus will do just that. In 1 Thessalonians Chapter 4 Verses 16-17 we read, *"For the Lord himself <u>shall descend from heaven</u> with a shout, with the voice of the archangel, and with the trump of God: and the dead in Christ shall rise first: <u>Then we which are alive and remain shall be caught up together with them in the clouds, to meet the Lord in the air</u>: and so shall we ever be with the Lord."* Verse 18 then states, *"Wherefore comfort one another with these words."*

Looking at this we see that this event when Jesus comes for His Church is described by catching up His Church to *"meet the Lord in the air."* Notice, this isn't what the Bible describes as Jesus Second Coming when He sets up His Kingdom on Earth. In Revelation 19 we see events of Jesus' return. We see that an army is following Him when He comes (v.14). That Army are all of those who died in Christ and who were Raptured seven years earlier. In Zachariah 14:4 we read that when the Messiah comes to earth to set up His Kingom He will set His feet on the Mount of Olives and it will split in two! It states, *"And his feet shall stand in that day upon the mount of Olives, which is before Jerusalem on the east, and the mount of Olives shall cleave in the midst thereof toward the east and toward the west, and there shall be a very great valley; and half of the mountain shall remove toward the north, and half of it toward the south."*

It's Clear

And so, it is clear that there are two different events coming to planet earth. One, when Christ, who promised He would prepare a place for His Church, comes to get His Church to take Her there. We also know that Scriptures states He meets them in the air (1 Thes 4:16-17) not on Earth. This is important because we also know that He will one day return to the planet itself with His armies following Him. He will set His feet on the planet and then set up His physical Kingdom and place Satan in the bottomless pit for 1,000 literal years (Rev 20:3).

The Quickly Approaching Rapture

Things Have to Happen First

Not only does the Bible clearly describe two specific differing events, i.e. the Rapture of the Church and the Return of Jesus, but it also describes many things that must happen before the latter. In other words, the Bible says a lot has to happen before His return, but the Bible also says that nothing has to happen before the Rapture. In Matthew 24 many events are listed as to what will occur before His return, but the entire Tribulation period is laid out in the book of Revelation. During that time-period Seven Seals, Seven Trumpets and Seven Vial judgments of God will come upon the planet and on those who inhabit it. Again, not to beat a dead horse, but if all these events have to happen but the Scripture tells Christians that the Lord could come at any moment, which is it?

Did God lie to mankind?

God forbid!

There are things that God can't do. He can't learn, because He knows all, and He certainly can't lie! So, if the Bible says a lot of things are going to happen on the planet during the Tribulation and before Jesus comes to set up His

The Quickly Approaching Rapture

Kingdom, but it also tells His people to be ready because He is coming for them at any moment, you can be sure of just that. He is coming at any moment for His Bride!

Matthew 24:44 states, *"Therefore be ye also ready: for in such an hour as ye think not the Son of man cometh."* Now, just think about this statement. Jesus says that He will come when people won't know. If the events of the Tribulation were occurring, reading Revelation, almost anyone with biblical knowledge could ascertain when Jesus would come back to set up His Kingdom. Jesus is obviously speaking about something else.

In Matthew 24:36 we read, *"But of that day and hour knoweth no man, no, not the angels of heaven, but my Father only."*

In Matthew 24:42 it is written, *"Watch therefore: for ye know not what hour your Lord doth come."*

In 1 Thessalonians 5:2-3 we read, *"For yourselves know perfectly that the day of the Lord so cometh as a thief in the night. For when they shall say, Peace and safety; then sudden destruction cometh upon them, as travail upon a woman with child; and they shall not*

The Quickly Approaching Rapture

escape." Note, the world will be saying peace and safety when the Lord comes for His Church. Does this sound like the Great Tribulation to you? Obviously not! When the Lord comes it will be as the passage in Luke 17 that says during the time when the Lord comes for His Church it will be like the days of Noah and Lot. People are partying and having a good old time when the judgment hits.

In Revelation 16:15 we see that warning once again. It states, **"Behold, I come as a thief. Blessed is he that watcheth, and keepeth his garments, lest he walk naked, and they see his shame."**

Chapter 8

Spiritual Eyes to See

Types and Shadows

While I have mentioned the parable of the ten virgins in Chapter One of this book it must be noted that there are other passages that relate to the Rapture from a "spiritual" context over a literal context. But before I jump too far forward I want to say that there are those in the Church who claim people like me see too many spiritual pictures and types. They claim we "over-spiritualize" things. Again, remember the lenses I have already mentioned. They come with a different lens and so I don't blame them for this critique. My hope is that they could see what some of us see, and we are not better or worse than they, we just use a different lens. I also want to point out that there are several things in the New Testament that the Scripture tells us not to be ignorant of. Things like God's not done with Israel (Rom 11:25) or the Gifts of the Holy Spirit (1 Cor 12:1) or the persecution and suffering of God's people (2 Cor 1:8) or even the Rapture of the Church

The Quickly Approaching Rapture

(1 Thes 4:13). These are all things the Bible tells us to not be ignorant of. And yet, looking at that list; God's not done with Israel, the Gifts of the Holy Spirit, God's people suffering and being persecuted, not always happy, healed and rich, and the Rapture of the Church are all things in which the different lenses see differently and where many Christians, and especially denominations, disagree.

There is another time when the Bible says we shouldn't be ignorant. This is found in 1 Corinthians 10:1-4. In this passage we see that an example of biblical types. It reads, *"Moreover, brethren, <u>I would not that ye should be ignorant</u>, how that all our fathers were under the cloud, and all passed through the sea; And were all baptized unto Moses in the cloud and in the sea; And did all eat the same spiritual meat; And did all drink the same spiritual drink: for they drank of that spiritual Rock that followed them: and that Rock was Christ."*

So, Jesus was a rock that Israel ate and drank from? Is the author over-spiritualizing? Absolutely not! This is a beautiful example of a picture in Scripture that is spiritually discerned. There are many examples of this type of thing in the Bible. Let me give you one example that blew my mind.

In Joshua Chapter 3 there is the story of the Children of Israel. We know that Moses had passed on and that Joshua was assigned to lead the Children of Israel. We know the backstory too. Moses, the first time recorded in Exodus 17:6 was told to strike the Rock so that water would come out of for the Israelites to drink. Knowing the passage in 1 Corinthians we just read that tells us Christ is that Rock, we then know that this is a picture of something. Moses is then told in Numbers 20 to speak to the Rock the second time the people needed water. However, Moses struck it again out of frustration, and God wasn't happy with what Moses had done. In Numbers 20:12 we read that because Moses didn't believe God enough to just speak to the Rock, God was not going to let Moses bring the Children of Israel into the promised land.

Stop and look at this so far. Among the Jewish people Moses is a massive figure. He represents the **Law** itself. If that be true think about the Gospel. If Jesus is that Rock (a picture) and Moses is the Law (a picture) then Jesus only had to be smitten or struck once for all! He was crucified for all. But, the Law just keeps striking, even though now Jesus merely needs to be spoken to. The smiting has already happened.

However, this entire picture doesn't stop there. Think about this. God said Moses, the Law, couldn't bring the Children of Israel into the promised land. Which, the promised land is a picture of the Christian life not Heaven, because we know battles still have to be fought and land still needs to be taken. But, in any case, the Law can't bring you into that life. It can bring you to it, just like Moses brought the Children of Israel right up next to it. But, it can't take you into it because the Law is a mirror and a school master to bring you to it.

Only Jesus can bring you into Salvation!

So, look at this. Who brought the Children of Israel into the promised land? The answer is Joshua!

What is Joshua's name in Hebrew? Jehoshua! The same name as our Lord.

Coincidence? I think not!

But, it doesn't stop there.

The Quickly Approaching Rapture

In Joshua Chapter 3 we see that when God brought Israel into the land it was Joshua leading the way. Where did they cross? Bethabara!!!

"Why is this important?" You ask.

Because this is the very spot where one day our JOSHUA, our Jehoshua, our Savior would be baptized. The very place the Children of Israel crossed and the place where Jesus was baptized are one in the same.

But, it doesn't stop there. Watch this!

God commands Joshua (Chapter 3) to have the Ark of the Covenant lead them into the promised land, but as soon as the priest's feet who are carrying the Ark touch the water it will dry up. Meaning the Jordan River will dry up and allow them all to cross over into the promised land. Verse 15 tells us it was also the time when the water was running deep and overflowing its banks. But as soon as the feet of the priests touched the water, it dried up.

In Joshua 3:16-17 we read, *"That the waters which came down from above stood and rose up upon an heap very far <u>from the city Adam</u>, that is beside Zaretan: and* *those that came down toward the sea of the plain, even the salt sea, failed, and were cut off."*

"So what?" You ask.

Look closer. Jehoshua takes his people into the promise land in the very place that our Jehoshua would one day be baptized. They cross over and the water dries up from the city of Adam to the salt sea.

What is another name for that sea?

Answer: The Dead Sea.

In other words, the waters dried up <u>from the city of Adam to the Dead Sea</u>. The city of Adam was about 19 miles away from the area. So why did God pick to dry the water up from there? Did God have a reason?

Yes!

They crossed over at Bethabara, and the water dried up from the city of Adam about 19 miles away all the way down to the Dead Sea. Again, this is the very spot Jesus would one day be baptized by John the Baptist, and we know that Jesus is the Very One who would <u>remove our sins all the way from Adam to death!</u>

The Quickly Approaching Rapture

Do you see the picture?

It's truly incredible if you have eyes to see! Jesus paid for our sins all the way from the fall of Adam to the curse of death!

You see, you could spend your whole life studying the Bible and never get to the end of it. Now, for those of you who say that's over-spiritualizing my heart breaks for you. I mean it. There are so many examples of this kind of imagery in the Scriptures, but I tell you, it does, in fact, take spiritual eyes to see them. For those who the Bible declares in 1 Corinthians Chapter 2 verse 13, *"Which things also we speak, **not in the words which man's wisdom teacheth**, but which **the Holy Ghost teacheth; comparing spiritual things with spiritual**."* It goes on to add in verse 14, *"**But the natural man receiveth not the things of the Spirit of God: for they are foolishness unto him**: neither can he know them, because they are **spiritually discerned**."* It concludes with verses 15-16, *"But he that is spiritual judgeth all things, yet he himself is judged of no man. For who hath known the mind of the Lord, that he may instruct him? but we have the mind of Christ."*

The Quickly Approaching Rapture

Many times, in Scripture a passage has a practical and a spiritual meaning, this really goes without saying. However, the question can then be asked, can the Bible be over-spiritualized? Sure, that goes without question. But, a similar question needs be asked as well. Can the Bible be under-spiritualized? The answer to that is just as the former, absolutely it can. The real question then becomes is there sufficient evidence to back the claims of one view over another?

Chapter 9

A Picture of the Rapture

The Seven Churches

In the book of Revelation there is a verse in Chapter 1 that lays out its entire outline. If you have previously read my book Mark*(s) of the Beast* then you know what I am probably going to say. In Chapter 1 verse 19 Jesus gives John the way to understand the book (Revelation), and how it will be organized. It states, *"Write the things which thou hast seen, and the things which are, and the things which shall be hereafter."*

Within this verse is the way you and I can also understand the book of Revelation. He tells John to *"write the things which thou has seen."* John had just seen the glorified resurrected Christ in all His Glory. He gives us that complete description in Chapter one. Then Jesus said to write, *"the things which are"* and from studying this out you will find that this is speaking of the Seven Churches that Jesus has John write seven letters to in Chapters 2 and 3. Then Jesus instructs John to write, *"the things which*

The Quickly Approaching Rapture

shall be hereafter." We know this to be Chapters 4-22 because that is the very line that starts Chapter 4 and everything within those following Chapters are future events.

However, it is that middle section I want to concentrate on for the purpose of this book. You see, the seven letters Jesus asks John to write to the seven Churches are critical in many ways. First, they were written for seven Churches of John's day. Those Churches were located in Asia Minor which is modern day Turkey. They were found along an old Roman postal route, and far from Jerusalem. These cities were close to Patmos where John was imprisoned. The thing is though, these seven Churches weren't the biggest or best. The reason these Churches were picked is somewhat a mystery. Still, Jesus picked them for a reason, or perhaps several reasons.

Since this book is about the Rapture I want to tell you why I chose to devote an entire section about these Churches and what it means to our study. First, please know these seven letters were written for seven literal Churches of John's day. I am not saying they aren't. These were Churches John may have been pastor to at some point.

The Quickly Approaching Rapture

But each letter is written in a way where Jesus communicates His thoughts specifically to them at that time.

Second, these letters are good for all Christians at all times. Within these letters, just like the rest of the Holy Scriptures, God gives you and I instruction on what to do and not to do in our Christian walk. There are warnings and lessons all through these letters for the Church in John's day, but also for the Church of any day, including ours.

The third dynamic I think these letters carry is that of the prophetic. When you analyze these letters out and see what each was dealing with, they seem to line up with the historical timeline of the Church. However, it must be noted that there is much overlap, and I believe at least four of these "Churches" are still on the planet today.

First, we see Ephesus (Rev 2:1). They were the Church that left their first love. This seems to line up pretty well with the early Church which transitioned around the late first to early second centuries.

The second Church is Smyrna (Rev 2:8), and this was the persecuted Church. This also seems to line up with

The Quickly Approaching Rapture

the next stage in Church history that led into a time of brutal persecution of Christians, especially in Rome, but really everywhere up to around the early 300's A.D.

Then we see Pergamos (Rev 2:12), and this is the Church that was worldly and began eating things sacrificed to idols. This seems to line up with the Roman Church which began with the edict of Constantine in the early 300's A.D. where idolatry and a partnership with earthly government began.

The next letter is written to the Church of Thyatira (Rev 2:18), and they were told that even though they did charitable acts and service they also allowed a false prophetess named Jezebel amongst them. This evil woman taught the Church to commit fornication and also eat things sacrificed to idols. When you look at the historical context this appears to line up with the general time which includes what we know as "the dark ages."

The next Church in Revelation (3:1) is Sardis. This Church had potential but faltered. This Church was told to strengthen what it did have or it would die. And, Jesus found that the works of this Church were not *"perfect before God."* Jesus also says not everyone would be

The Quickly Approaching Rapture

judged, and he explains that there are some within this Church that are worthy for His Kingdom. This seems to line up with the time known as the Protestant Reformation. Yes, it was good what Martin Luther did in breaking away from the mother Church which was suppressing the Word and not holding to its truth. No, it wasn't good all the atrocities, denominations, and events that transpired as a result.

The sixth Church on the list in Revelation (3:7) is Philadelphia. Jesus had only good things to say about this Church, but He also said they had little strength but they kept to His Word and didn't deny His name. This seems to line up with the time of the Great Awakenings and vast numbers of missionaries and Pastors that sacrificed for the Word of God and the Gospel.

The last Church is Laodicea (Rev 3:14). This Church was all about themselves. In fact, the name means "Ruled by the People". This Church thought they were rich and in need of nothing, but Jesus told them that they were "wretched, miserable, poor, blind and naked." If you didn't see it already it appears to be a no brainer that many calling themselves Christians in the modern time seem to line up with this. Ruled by self, not God or His Word, and more worried about money or riches over being righteous or obedient.

Last Four

For the sake of this study I want to point out again that there is overlap and at least four of these prophetic Churches, I contend, are still on the planet today.

Thyatira

First we know that the historical Church (Thyatira), which doesn't just include the Catholic Church, but certainly does to a large extent, and they are still here on the planet. What does God say to that Church about the Rapture? In Revelation 2:24-25 after saying that even though the Church was charitable and did acts of service they also accepted a woman who was a false prophetess. This woman taught them to practice idolatry. God says He gave her time to repent (Rev 2:21). But the letter does go on to say that not all in this Church will be judged. Verses 24-25 states, ***"But unto you I say, and unto the rest in Thyatira, as many as have not this doctrine, and which have not known the depths of Satan, as they speak; I will*** *put upon you none other burden. <u>But that which ye have already hold fast till I come.</u>"*

So, if this a historical Church the Bible says some within it, who have not fallen to idolatry by this false female prophetess, will be saved at His coming. However, many will not be saved because of their idolatry and their lack of true repentance.

It must be noted that the Catholic Church, in general looks at eschatology and end times events, mostly through an Amillennial lens with a few small variations.

Sardis

The next Church, Sardis, which lines up with the Protestant Reformation, also has a promise. Jesus reminds them to *"remember therefore how thou hast received and heard"* (Rev 3:3). He then instructs them to repent. If they don't repent He says, *"I will come on thee as a thief, and thou shalt not know what hour I will come upon thee."*

This seems to be a clear indication of the verses previously mentioned in this book concerning the Rapture of the Church. This Church needs to repent or they will not make it (*I will come on thee as a thief, and thou shalt not know what hour I will come upon thee*).

But, let's be clear, Jesus also says there are a *"few"* in this Church who are worthy to escape. In Revelation 3:4 it states, *"Thou hast a few names even in Sardis which have not defiled their garments; and they shall walk with me in white: for they are worthy."*

When you study this out further you will find that many of the Protestant Reformation denominations also tend to look at eschatology mostly through an Amillennial lens.

Laodicea

I will skip Philadelphia right now and go straight to Laodicea. After all, the church in Laodicea wouldn't have a problem getting a place of prominence and cutting in line. This starts with a simple examination of the name of the city itself. Laodicea means "ruled by the people" and this church certainly was. Jesus has nothing good to say about this group. He tells them they are neither hot nor cold but lukewarm, and because of this He is going to, *"spue thee out of my mouth"* (Rev 3:16). Think about that. Jesus is going to *"spue"* or vomit them out.

He goes on to rebuke them because this Church thinks they are rich and in need of nothing but Jesus tells them they are actually horrible poor and impoverished. Revelation 3:17 states, *"Because thou sayest, I am rich, and increased with goods, and have need of nothing; and knowest not that thou art wretched, and miserable, and poor, and blind, and naked."*

Jesus then says the only answer for this church to turn to Him is to *"buy of me gold tried in fire."*

Let me just stop for a second. First, this church, when looking prophetically with the church it lines up with, it sure seems to parallel what has been going on in Christianity over the last one hundred years or so. A self-centered, signs and wonders seeking, wealth focused, me church, has been steadily growing. Just think about the amount of huge churches in the United States alone that are full of thousands of people focused on "getting their blessing" or "claiming their riches." Think about all the churches that are focused on pleasing people over pleasing God. I won't belabor it too much, but chances are, if you are reading this book, you know exactly what I am talking about.

It's really sad the way so many modern Churches have replaced the Word of God with entertainment, activity and programs. Many of these people-pleasing, money-focused, entertainment-centered "churches" are really nothing of the sort. They have very little of the elements that are supported in Scripture as to what a group of gathered believers should do or why they should even do it. Many times, their prayers are self-focused, and their "messages" are not really sermons, but rather, self-help and positive-thinking speeches focused on signs, blessings, and often times on getting stuff.

Where did the Word of God go? It's ironic when I talk to some in these movements they say, "my pastor teaches the Bible." But, they don't understand that an opinionated teaching full of stories and anecdotes, usually laced with exaggeration, and very few Bible verses sprinkled in, out of context in many cases when they are, is not teaching the Bible! The systematic teaching of God's Word is desperately needed in this modern church, but they are too worried, it seems, about getting more people in their church, entertaining them, lathering them up in some emotional experience, generating signs and wonders, and building their own little religious Hollywood. Thus, the answer for this kind of church echoes in the words of Jesus to the Laodiceans, *"As many as I love, I rebuke and chasten: be zealous therefore, and repent"* (v.19).

His discipline is coming, and if those with this kind of "Christianity" do not repent they will endure fiery trial. That trial comes in the form of the Tribulation because they were never really believers, but rather, religious people worshiping a false self-made Jesus. Verse 20 states, **"Behold, I stand at the door, and knock: if any man hear my voice, and open the door, I will come in to him, and will sup with him, and he with me."**

Notice, for this church, the door is shut. But, Jesus is knocking on it. He warns them that if they don't repent fire will come in the form of His counsel. He tells them if they don't repent He is going to puke them out.

When you study this out further you find that a large number of churches that would fit this profile often view Scripture through a Postmillennial lens, but not always and this is important. This movement often teaches the "Kingdom Now" theology or that Christians are going to take over the world and usher in a time of a golden age and then Christ will come. But, there are also those in this group that have a Premillennial belief but are still caught up in all the rest of the junk.

The Quickly Approaching Rapture

In stark contrast to the closed door of the Laodicea, the Church in Philadelphia has nothing within it that Jesus rebukes, and He Himself says, ***"I know thy works: behold, I have set before thee an <u>open door</u>, and no man can shut it"*** (Rev 3:8a).

This is a loving Church, and the name "Philadelphia" literally means "Brotherly Love." This Church certainly lines up with the time of the First and Second Great Awakenings historically. We still see the fruit of men like Jonathan Edwards, George Whitefield, and Hudson Taylor. Men who sacrificed for the Gospel, and a revival that spread across the world. I believe this continued on into the 1900's with what is commonly known as "The Jesus Movement" that started in the late 1960's and was quite an astonishing move of God.

When looking at this Church in the Bible from a prophetic understanding, it is still here on the planet today. It is present in many churches which hold to the Word of God. Their focus is on the teaching of the Word of God and equipping the people of God to live obedient and surrendered lives. They generally teach believers to love God and each other, and to evangelize and make disciples.

The Quickly Approaching Rapture

They are generally bold in their faith and quite active in their communities. This group, just like the Philadelphia Church, have a simple recipe. Jesus Himself tells us what that recipe is. He tells Philadelphia that because they have, *"Kept my word, and has not denied my name"*, that He, Jesus would do something amazing for them. Verse 10b of Revelation 3 states, *"I also will keep thee <u>from the hour of temptation</u>, which shall come upon all the world, to try them that dwell upon the earth."*

The word there for "temptation" according to *Strong's*, is "Peirasmos" in the Greek. It means, "a putting of proof" or "discipline" or "adversity". I want to note that this is a different word than is used in John 16:33 when Jesus told His disciples, *"These things I have spoken unto you, that in me ye might have peace. In the world ye shall have <u>tribulation</u>: but be of good cheer; I have overcome the world."*

Some have argued that the above verse containing the word *"tribulation"* is proof Jesus is telling the Church they will have to endure part or all of the Great Tribulation to come. That's just not true. First, the context doesn't fit. Jesus is telling them that they will have trouble in the world

The Quickly Approaching Rapture

but not to worry because He has overcome the world. If He was talking about the Tribulation, this would make absolutely no sense. Second, the word used for ***"tribulation"*** in this passage is "Thlipsis" and *Strong's* says it means "pressure" or "anguished" or "persecution" or "trouble". And, in the context we know that Christians will experience those things in this world. But they will not experience God's Wrath in the form of the ***"hour of temptation, which shall come upon the world, to try them that dwell upon the earth"*** (Rev 3:10).

Jesus then immediately adds in Verse 11, ***"Behold, I come quickly: hold fast which thou hast, that no man take thy crown."***

Do you see the significance of this?

Jesus tells this faithful Church that because they have held to His Word and didn't deny His name, that He would keep them from the Tribulation. He tells this Church that He is coming quickly. He also says that because they have held to His Word and didn't deny His name, He is opening a ***"door"*** for them that no man can shut. He states that because of this holding to His Word He will also keep them from the ***"hour of temptation"*** that is coming upon

The Quickly Approaching Rapture

the entire world for the purpose of trying those on the planet. That "open door" also lines up with Revelation 4:1, which many like me believe is a clear picture of the Rapture. It states, *"After this I looked, and, behold, <u>a door was opened in heaven</u>: and the first <u>voice</u> which I heard was as it were <u>of a trumpet</u> talking with me; which said, <u>Come up hither</u>, and I will shew thee things which must be hereafter"* (Rev 4:1).

If you see this passage in Revelation 4 it mentions the door, it mentions a loud voice, and it mentions a trumpet, just like 1 Thessalonians 4:16 which is speaking about the Rapture. You also see that this is when John is taken to Heaven while writing Revelation. This takes place after the letters to the Churches, and when you look at the overall timeline, it fits prophetically as the end of the "Church age". There is so much more to this study. I encourage you to examine this yourself.

However, I do want <u>you</u> to go back and re-read Revelation 3:7-13 and examine what I have said.

Go ahead, I'll just wait over here until you're done.

Do you see it now?

The Quickly Approaching Rapture

When examining these Churches through a prophetic understanding it certainly seems to have some kind of alignment with the four largest Christian groups on the planet now. For those of you who think I am reading too much into it or over-spiritualizing, that's where we will just have to agree to disagree. For those of you who do have eyes to see, I hope you indeed can see the lesson in all of this. Jesus is coming for His Church soon. He is coming for those who are faithful. He is coming for those hold to His Word. He is coming for those that don't deny His name. He's on the doorstep and soon that door will open for those are truly His.

I wonder—are you His?

Chapter 10

To Disappear or Not Disappear?

Conventional Teaching

For those of us who do believe in a Rapture it has often been taught that when the Rapture occurs all believers, and the children of believers, will simply disappear. This is what I have believed for many years myself. However, in this chapter I am going to look at two possibilities. First, I will look at what the Scripture says about all believers disappearing at the Rapture. I will show you passages that might suggest this to be true. But, I am also going to examine the theory that instead of disappearing, all believers will simply fall "dead" right where they are. Not that we will die in a conventional sense, but that at the Rapture Jesus will take our souls and exchange our old bodies for a perfect eternal body all at the same moment.

Going into this Chapter I want to be completely transparent. I do not know which one of these things will occur, or if another option like spontaneous combustion could be true (I'm only mostly joking). But, I can actually see evidence for at least two options in Scripture. Now, the reason I want to include this Chapter in this book is to be responsible when it comes to the Word of God, and to leave behind a resource for those who are left behind after the Rapture.

If the Rapture occurs and we all disappear—great!

But, if the Rapture occurs and it looks like a pandemic or other weird or strange sudden massive deaths of believers, or even something totally different, I want those left behind to know that this was indeed the event known as "The Rapture of the Church" and not "Mother Earth" protecting herself or a pandemic, or a new weapon, or whatever.

Can You Imagine?

I can just imagine the lies that will be told no matter what happens to all of us Christians. Those lies will be epic. It was aliens! It was disease! It was… fill in the blank. No matter what happens I want those reading this book during the Tribulation to know that there is the possibility of our bodies being left behind or disappearing or who knows, and they shouldn't believe the lies being told in response.

Disappearing Act

The Quickly Approaching Rapture

First, let's look at the possibility of all believers disappearing at the event known as The Rapture of the Church. Like I said, this is what I had always believed, and there is Scripture to support it. In the first section of this book I went through all the verses that had the word "Harpazo" in them. One of those such verses had to do with the story of Philip and the Ethiopian eunuch. Philip witness to him, baptizes him, and then Philip is "Harpazoed" the same word as Rapture, nineteen miles away from where he baptized the new convert. Acts 8:39 states, ***"And when they were come up out of the water, the Spirit of the Lord <u>caught away</u> Philip."***

When looking at this verse it seems to be a slam dunk for those who believe that when we are taken in the Rapture we will disappear. After all, Philip did, and he was transported 19 miles away to the city of ***"Azotus"*** (v.40).

However, Philip wasn't done with his earthly body. He didn't go to Heaven, and He wasn't transformed or "changed" like Scripture states those in the Rapture will be. Still, I can see comparing this to the Rapture. It is the same word used in the Greek.

The Quickly Approaching Rapture

Another passage that seems to support the disappearance of believers is one that will actually be used to support both theories. It's the most famous passage concerning the Rapture and I have already quoted it in this book. It's found in 1 Thessalonians 4 verse 16-17. It states, *"For the Lord himself shall descend from heaven with a shout, with the voice of the archangel, and with the trump of God: <u>and the dead in Christ shall rise first</u>: Then we which are alive and remain <u>shall be caught up together with them in the clouds, to meet the Lord in the air</u>: and so shall we ever be with the Lord."*

The common understanding of this, at least when it comes to the theory that we will disappear, is that at the Rapture Jesus will bring the souls of those who have died and give them new bodies made from their old bodies, but transformed somehow into holy bodies, and that the rest of those alive on the planet, who are His, will have their earthly bodies changed into heavenly bodies and thus, disappear.

Again, this is what I believed for a long time, but now I am not sure. The reason I say I'm not sure is actually three-fold. First, why would we need our bodies that are made of flesh even if they are changed? We know that nothing good dwells in the flesh (Rom 7:8). Second, why wouldn't we just discard the old and put on the new? Third, Scripture could actually be saying that we will put off our old bodies and put on new ones.

The last reason is the only one that really matters. When it comes to Scripture I can see how someone could say we would disappear by being transformed. But, I can also see where we leave these bodies behind.

Fall Where We Are

What if our bodies stay behind? When I look at the Scriptures I can see this happening. First, we know that when Paul talks about a certain *"man"* visiting the Third Heaven he states, ***"whether in the body, I cannot tell; or whether out of the body, I cannot tell: God knoweth; such a <u>one caught up</u> to the third heaven"*** (2 Cor 12:2b).

In this passage Paul, who is most likely the *"man"* caught up, doesn't know if it was in the body or out of the body. This is relevant because the word used there for "caught up" is "Harpazo" and, unlike Philip, Paul entered Heaven.

The Quickly Approaching Rapture

Of course, this is just one passage, but it led me to look closer at others. I then went back to 1 Thessalonians Chapter 4. I looked at the order of things and how it was written. I had always thought Jesus would bring those who have died in faith back and somehow gather their DNA from all over the world and transform them into new bodies, then do the same thing to those who are alive in Him. But, what if it's saying something different? What if it's just giving us the order of things?

Paul writes to the Thessalonians so that they wouldn't be troubled. First, he didn't want them to be troubled about those who went on before them in the Lord. He states in 1 Thessalonians 4:13-14, *"But I would not have you to be ignorant, brethren, <u>concerning them which are asleep, that ye sorrow not, even as others which have no hope.</u> For if we believe that Jesus died and rose again, even so them also which sleep in Jesus will God bring with him."*

So, Jesus will bring those who have died in Christ with Him. He then says in verse 15, *"For this we say unto you by the word of the Lord, that we which are alive and* *remain unto the coming of the Lord <u>shall not prevent them which are asleep.</u>"*

From this verse another passage seems to make even more sense In 2 Corinthians 5:6-8 we read, *"Therefore we are always confident, <u>knowing that, whilst we are at home in the body, we are absent from the Lord:</u> (For we walk by faith, not by sight:) We are confident, <u>I say, and willing rather to be absent from the body, and to be present with the Lord</u>."*

So, we know that all believers in Jesus Christ, as soon as they pass on they are in Heaven with Jesus. So, looking again at 1 Thessalonians 4:16-17 when it says, *"the dead in Christ shall rise first: Then we which are alive and remain shall be caught up together with them in the clouds, to meet the Lord in the air: and so shall we ever be with the Lord."*

Could it not be an order of things currently?

Is Paul telling these individuals not to fret because those who die in Christ go to be with Him immediately and our Rapture or His Return is not preventing that. In other words, the dead in Christ shall rise first, which is currently happening, and then the Rapture.

Or, another thing this passage could be simply saying is that at the moment He comes for His Church the dead in Christ will receive an incorruptible body, but it wouldn't have to be made from the old one, would it?

I know this might be confusing but stay with me. What I am saying is this doesn't necessarily say that those "dead in Christ" will get new bodies made from the old, and it doesn't specifically say we who are alive when He comes will keep our current bodies which will be somehow cleansed and transformed.

Let's look at the 1 Corinthians 15 passage because it has some interesting things to say. He is discussing the first Adam (who was the first man created) and the Last Adam, which is Jesus Christ. He is talking about natural things and spiritual things and comparing and contrasting them. In Verse 50 he writes, *"Now this I say, brethren, that flesh and blood cannot inherit the kingdom of God; neither doth corruption inherit incorruption."* He then immediately goes into Rapture speak in verse 51, *"Behold, I shew you a mystery; We shall not all sleep, but we shall*

all be changed, In a moment, in the twinkling of an eye, at the last trump: for the trumpet shall sound, and the dead shall be raised incorruptible, and we shall be changed."

Let's unpack what he just said. He writes, **"*flesh and blood cannot inherit the kingdom of God*"** nor does **"*corruption inherit incorruption."*** He also states, **"*and the dead shall be raised incorruptible, and we shall be changed."*** Which, makes total sense whether we are completely changed or get a completely new body leaving the old behind, we know that something drastic has to happen for us to enter Heaven.

But then he goes on to say even more. He states in Verses 53-54, **"*For this corruptible must <u>put on incorruption</u>, and this mortal must <u>put on immortality</u>. So, when this corruptible shall have <u>put on incorruption</u>, and this mortal shall have <u>put on immortality</u>, then shall be brought to pass the saying that is written, Death is swallowed up in victory."***

When looking at that phrase **"*put on"*** it is the word "Enduo" in the Greek according to *Strong's*. It means, "sinking into a garment" or "to invest with clothing" or to

The Quickly Approaching Rapture

"clothe"(G1746). That seems to me like putting on something new rather than the transformation of something old. If I am wearing old clothes I must take them off before I put on new clothes right? I know some of you think your funny and yes, I know I could put them over the old, but not in the case of our flesh. Back in verse 50 it clearly states, *"flesh and blood cannot inherit the kingdom of God"* nor does *"corruption inherit incorruption."*

So, all I'm saying is that covering old clothes with new won't work in the Kingdom of God. We need new clothes, new flesh, new bodies.

My logical question is simply why would God be interested in saving the old wicked flesh? Even by transforming it…

Wouldn't we need to change our clothes?

In other words, if this theory holds true, the transformation or *"changed"* that happens to us as described in 1 Corinthians 15:51 is not a disappearing act, but instead the old body will be left and the new will be received. That verse reads, *"Behold, I shew you a mystery; We shall not all sleep, but we shall all be <u>changed</u>."*

The Quickly Approaching Rapture

The word there for *"changed"* is "Allasso" in the Greek and according to *Strong's* it means "to make different" (G236). It comes from the root word "allos" which *Strong's* says means, "else that is, different" or "other" (G243).

So, whatever we put on at the Rapture is different, it's other. Again, I am not here to convince you one way or another. I'm not even convinced myself. I am simply laying out a case for both. We might disappear. Or, I also see Scripture that could be pointing to a changing of clothing, that is, a new body and the old one is left behind. At the time of writing this book I can honestly say I just don't know, and maybe we won't know until it happens. Whether we disappear or our bodies fall where they are, I want those who are left behind to not be fooled. If millions "die" around the globe or if millions "disappear", my hope is that many will recognize what is really going on and repent immediately and give themselves to Christ. Of course, my greatest hope is that they would do that right now, but there are some in the Tribulation that may go hunting for literature to explain things, and I hope this book helps!

Chapter 11

Apostasy or Apost-a-see-ya?

Falling Away or Taking Away?

There is another passage in Scripture that has to do with the Rapture that is found in 2 Thessalonians Chapter 2. It is a section of Scripture where Paul the Apostle, under the inspiration of the Holy Spirit, is writing to the Church in Thessalonica. It seems as if someone has been telling them that the Day of the Lord has come, which means they have missed the Rapture.

We will be looking at this passage because I believe it's important to understand what is being said in light of a new theory that has grown in popularity in recent years. The traditional view states that in the last days there will a great "Apostasy" when many will depart from the faith and go their own way. A second camp now claims that the word "Apostasy" or "Falling Away" is really the Rapture, and it describes the Church being taken away. I am going to look at both theories after I give you some overview of each, and then explain which theory I hold to and why.

The Quickly Approaching Rapture

Traditional View

Over the years this passage has usually been translated that Paul is encouraging the Church there in Thessalonica that the Day of the Lord hasn't come because the *"falling away"* or *"apostasy"* hasn't occurred, nor has the *"man of sin"* or Anti-Christ been revealed. This falling away is often thought of as a time of heresy and people leaving the Christian faith. Paul makes it clear that because the Church hasn't seen these things they can be sure they are not in the *"Day of Christ"* (v.2), which is also the Day of the Lord, also known as the Tribulation. Paul also tells them that there is someone, a *"he"* (v.7) who will not allow the *"son of perdition"* (v.3) to be *"revealed"* (v.6) until *"he be taken out of the way"* (v.7). This "he" is sometimes thought of being the Holy Spirit or the work of the Holy Spirit in the Church, but I will come back to this when I explain this view in greater detail.

The New Theory

In recent years the common understanding of this passage has been challenged by a new theory. The change happened, as I can see, for a few different reasons, but mostly it hinges on the word in Verse 3 which is usually translated "Apostasy" or "Falling Away" or "Departure".

The Quickly Approaching Rapture

Those who hold to this new theory believe that the word "Apostasy" is actually a departure of the Church, or the Rapture.

The Passage

To understand where each of these theories stand and why they believe what they do we need to look at what is being said in 2 Thessalonians Chapter 2. We will first look at the first four verses, *"Now we beseech you, brethren, by the coming of our Lord Jesus Christ, and by our gathering together unto him" (v.1).*

First thing I need to address is in verse one there is certainly a distinction between the *"gathering together unto him"* and the *"coming of our Lord Jesus Christ."* Again, these are two distinct events.

Verse 2 reads, *"That ye be not soon shaken in mind, or be troubled, neither by spirit, nor by word, nor by letter as from us, as that the day of Christ is at hand."*

Here we see Paul is trying to calm them down and let them know the "Day of Christ" which is also the "Day of the Lord" has not started (Rev 6:16-17). This is the time also known as the Tribulation, and this group was worried they were in it, and somehow missed the *"gathering together unto him."*

The Quickly Approaching Rapture

Paul then tells them to not believe the lies, and that there are things that will occur in the time-period just before the Tribulation and during it, that clearly have not occurred. In other words, Paul is telling them to relax because the clear indication of the Day of the Lord is an apostasy and the subsequent reveal of the Anti-Christ. He writes, *"Let no man deceive you by any means: for that day shall not come, except there come a <u>falling away</u> first, and <u>that man of sin be revealed</u>, the son of perdition; Who opposeth and exalteth himself above all that is called God, or that is worshipped; so that he as God sitteth in the temple of God, shewing himself that he is God" (v.3-4).*

Compare and Contrast

This is the section where the two theories do not agree. The traditional theory believes that the *"falling away"* in verse 3 is a last days departure from the faith, but the new theory suggests the *"falling away"* is better translated "departure" and this is actually the Rapture of the Church.

If you look at the timeline of what the new theory suggests, it <u>does</u> seem to fit the timeline of those of us who believe in a Pre-Tribulation Rapture. After all, a "departure" of the Church does also seem to fit what verses

6-7 say about the rise of the Anti-Christ and the "He" being the Holy Spirit's work in the Church, has to be removed before the Anti-Christ can be revealed. It reads, *"And now ye know what withholdeth that he might be revealed in his time. For the mystery of iniquity doth already work: only he who now letteth will let, until he be taken out of the way."*

The New King James translates it this way, *"⁶And now you know what is restraining, that he may be revealed in his own time. ⁷ For the mystery of lawlessness is already at work; only He who now restrains will do so until He is taken out of the way."* (NKJ)

Notice the capital "H" on "He" both times in verse 7? This is different than the "he" in verse 6 which speaks of the Anti-Christ, but verse 7 is often understood to be the Holy Spirit, as previously mentioned.

The New theory believes that this is a retelling of verse 3 of the "departure" of the Church, and when looking at it closely it does appear to be the case, if, and only if, the word for "falling away" is in fact, "departure" and represents the Rapture of the Church.

Problems With the New Theory

The Quickly Approaching Rapture

The new theory of this passage has two glaring problems. First, Paul, in his opening line is talking to the Church about the Rapture, the *"gathering together unto him."* Why then would he encourage them in that, the Rapture wouldn't occur until the Rapture happens?

What do you mean by that? You ask.

Well, simply this. If Paul is talking about the Rapture and then verse 3 is talking about the Rapture it doesn't really make sense. For the sake of example, I will place the word "Rapture" in both places to see if it makes sense. Note, I am not changing Scripture, I am using this as an illustration.

"¹Now we beseech you, brethren, by the coming of our Lord Jesus Christ, and by (the Rapture), *² That ye be not soon shaken in mind, or be troubled, neither by spirit, nor by word, nor by letter as from us, as that the day of Christ is at hand.³ Let no man deceive you by any means: for that day shall not come, except there come a* (Rapture) *first, and that man of sin be revealed, the son of perdition."*

Do you see the problem? It doesn't make sense to tell them not to worry that the Rapture had come because the Rapture would have to happen first.

The Quickly Approaching Rapture

The second problem with this new theory is the word used for *"falling away"* in the Greek language. That word, according to *Strong's* is "Apostasia" which simply means, "defection from the truth" or "falling away" or "forsake" (G646). The root words associated with this word are "Aphistemi", which means to, "remove" or "instigate to revolt" to "desert" or even to "withdraw self" (G868). The other root word is "Apostasion" which means to "divorce" or "divorcement" (G647).

This word "Apostasia" is only used twice in Scripture. Once in the verse in 2 Thessalonians Chapter 2 and once in Acts 21:21 where it reads, *"And they are informed of thee, that thou teachest all the Jews which are among the Gentiles to forsake Moses, saying that they ought not to circumcise their children, neither to walk after the customs."*

So, if you look at this passage in Acts the word "Apostasia" is used to mean "forsake", and this is the only other time besides 2 Thessalonians 2:3 it is used. Not only that, but when you look at the word and its roots it is related to "divorce" or to "instigate a revolt" and to "withdraw self". Which, if you know what the Rapture is, while it might be a divorcement from the world, Christians are already not of this world. If it is a revolt the Rapture certainly isn't that. And if it is a withdrawing of self, that is clearly not the Rapture because Jesus comes to withdraw us. Then, when you look at the meaning of the original word you also see that it means a "defection from the truth" or "falling away" or to "forsake". And, the only other time this word is used in the Bible is to mean to "forsake" someone.

Overall, while the timeline would line up with the Bible, the new theory doesn't hold up to the test of the Word of God itself nor of the meaning of the word the Holy Spirit chose to utilize in this letter.

The Problem With the Traditional Theory

There is also an issue with the traditional theory of 2 Thessalonians 2. It is related to the theology that many of us hold to. Namely, that a true born-again believer, sealed by the Spirt of God, cannot lose their salvation. And, when you read verse 3 it seems to indicate that in the time-period leading up to the Tribulation there are going to be many "Christians" who leave the faith and appear to lose their salvation. The "Great Apostasy" as it is referred to by many is a time when believers will apparently walk away from their faith in Christ. Now, if you are one who believes that

The Quickly Approaching Rapture

a Christian <u>can</u> lose their salvation you are probably saying, "I see no problem." But, before you get too comfortable in that position let's look closer at this because what I think is actually being said here is that there will be those in the last days propagating a false Christianity. This group will be large I believe, and I think it will come from different "kinds" of so-called Christianity. I also believe the problem for the traditional theory only exists if you think fake Christians ever had salvation in the first place. Remember, Judas himself was called "friend" by Jesus, and he spent a few years by Jesus' side without other disciples even suspecting his true heart, which was focused on money and power. Not only that, but in 1 John 2:19 we read, ***"They went out from us, but they were not of us; for if they had been of us, they would no doubt have continued with us: but they went out, that they might be made manifest that they were not all of us."***

    My opinion is that there are several passages in Scripture that tell us that a born-again believer is sealed (Eph 4:30, John 10:28-29, John 5:24, Jude 1:24, Heb 7:25, Rom 8:38-39). Also, there are passages that clearly state that some who look like believers are not believers (Matt 7:21, 1 Jn 2:19, Rev 3:15-16, Luke 6:46, Rom 16:17-18).

The Quickly Approaching Rapture

Logically, when studying out the Omniscient All-Knowing God we serve, and understanding, at least to some degree, His sovereignty over all things, it's hard to believe He would "seal" anyone who He knows down the road at some future time, was going to leave the faith. It just doesn't make sense. Nor does it make sense that a Christian, who was saved by Grace alone through faith, and not of works, could now somehow be unsaved by works. We know from Scripture that God knows the beginning from the end, and I don't think it's a far stretch to say many who claim to be Christians were never sealed by God, because God knows their hearts, their true motivations, and every second of their entire lives.

But, because I want to be responsible I also say this. I know God isn't going to drag anyone into Heaven that doesn't want to be there. He's God, and He knows all, and I don't want to put Him in my created box. However, from studying the Scripture I believe because He is all-knowing, it really solves the issue. I don't know who's saved for sure, but God certainly does. And, He will seal those that He seals.

Is it a Falling Away if They Never Had It?

The Quickly Approaching Rapture

Over the years some Bible scholars have suggested that the "falling away" is really referring to the "world" and not necessarily the Church. These same scholars believe the rebellion (the world) will have against God in the last days is what is being spoken of here. While this is certainly going to happen as well, and is already happening, I don't necessarily agree that this is what is being communicated in verse 3. I think it is clear that Paul's writings in First and Second Timothy line up with a last days rebellion among those who call themselves believers in Christ but are most likely "Christian" by name only.

1 Timothy 4:1-3 states, *"Now the Spirit speaketh expressly, that <u>in the latter times</u> <u>some shall depart from the faith, giving heed to seducing spirits, and doctrines of devils</u>; Speaking lies in hypocrisy; having their conscience seared with a hot iron; Forbidding to marry, and commanding to abstain from meats, which God hath created to be received with thanksgiving of them which believe and know the truth."*

In 2 Timothy Chapter 3 verses 1-5 we read, *"This know also, that in <u>the last days perilous times shall come</u>. For men shall be lovers of their own selves, covetous, boasters, proud, blasphemers, disobedient to parents,*

The Quickly Approaching Rapture

unthankful, unholy, Without natural affection, trucebreakers, false accusers, incontinent, fierce, despisers of those that are good, Traitors, heady, highminded, <u>lovers of pleasures more than lovers of God; Having a form of godliness, but denying the power</u> thereof: from such turn away."

In 2 Timothy 4:3-4 it is written, *"For <u>the time will come</u> when they <u>will not endure sound doctrine</u>; but after their own lusts shall they heap to themselves teachers, having itching ears; And they shall turn away their ears from the truth, and shall be turned unto fables."*

In looking at these passages it's clear that the Bible indicates that people will be able to claim to be believers, and yet be willing participants in evil doctrines that are not lined up with the true teachings of Christ. In 1 Timothy 4 we read that in the latter times there will be those that *"<u>shall depart</u> from the faith giving heed to seducing spirits, and doctrines of devils"* (v.1). It must be noted that the word used for "shall depart" is the aforementioned "Aphistemi" (G868) which is one of the root words of "Apostasia". Remember it means to "instigate a revolt" or "withdraw self." Whatever this is, it's an attack on true Christianity, and I don't believe it's proof of true believers losing salvation and plucking themselves out of the Father's Hand.

We also see in this same passage that some in this last days rebellion will forbid some to marry and *"abstain"* from meats. These seem to be harsh religious rules that would be dictated to those who follow their doctrine.

In 2 Timothy 3 we saw that some in the last days will be *"lovers of pleasure rather than lovers of God"* (v.4) and they will be, *"having a <u>form</u> of godliness, but denying the power"* (v.5). The word there for "form", according to *Strong's* is "Morphosis" (G3446) which means "appearance" it comes from the root word "Morphoo" (G3445) which means to "fashion" which comes from the root "Morphe" (G3444) which means to "shape" or "form". In other words, this individuals take on the appearance, or morph into some kind of godly costume. It's a show for them.

But, the verse continues to say that they have a form of godliness but *"denying the power."* The word *"power"* comes from the Greek word "Dunamis", which is where we get our word dynamite. It's power alright, but in biblical context *Strong's* says it's "specifically miraculous power" (G1411).

The Quickly Approaching Rapture

And what do these false Christians do with this power? The word there for "denying" is "Arneomai" which means "to contradict" or to "reject" or even to "refuse" (G720). Here's where it gets really interesting. One of the root words associated with this word for "denying" is the word "Hreho" which *Strong's* says has the "idea of pouring forth" and also "to utter that is to speak or say" to "command" or to "make" (G4483). So, whoever these people are they deny or "contradict" or "reject" or even "refuse" the real "miraculous power" of God. They seem to exchange it for their own made up power, or worse yet, power from evil forces. They also then seem to "utter" or "speak" or "command" in their efforts of doing so. Verse 4 of 2 Timothy 3 says they also are *"lovers of pleasures more than lovers of God"*. Meaning, they are focused and desire the lusts of this world over the love of God.

Finally there is the passage in 2 Timothy 4:3-4 which says that in the last days some are not going to *"endure sound doctrine"* and they will go after *"their own lusts"* and that they will then *"heap to themselves teachers having itching ears"* and that finally *"they will turn away their ears from the truth and shall be turned unto fables."*

The Quickly Approaching Rapture

The words there for "sound doctrine" simply mean healthy instruction. Where does that kind of Instruction come from? Hebrews 4:12 states, *"For the word of God is quick, and powerful, and sharper than any two-edged sword, piercing even to the dividing asunder of soul and spirit, and of the joints and marrow, and is a discerner of the thoughts and intents of the heart."*

True, healthy instruction. comes from God's Word and is confirmed by His Spirit. However, these in the last days aren't going to want this. Instead they *"heap to themselves teachers"* that tell them what they want to hear. They will flock to those who will tell them the things that line up with their lust for pleasures. They are going to turn away from the true Word of God and dive into *"fables"*. The word for "fables" is "Muthos" which means "a tale, that is, fiction" (G3454). In other words, they have traded truth for a lie.

In Romans 16 we see that God instructs Paul how to handle these types of fake believers. In verse 17-18 we read, *"Now I beseech you, brethren, mark them which cause divisions and offences contrary to the doctrine which ye have learned; and avoid them. For they that are such serve not our Lord Jesus Christ, but their own belly;*

The Quickly Approaching Rapture

and by good words and fair speeches deceive the hearts of the simple."

The Theory I Hold To

While studying this topic out over the last few years I have come to the conclusion that when 2 Thessalonians is talking about a *"falling away"* or "apostasy" it is talking about just that. In the last days an "apostasy" or rebellion, will occur. There will be many who put on a costume of godliness but will be nothing of the sort. However, the real danger is they are probably going to offer a message that is far more profitable and tempting for the lost, and it will be received over the message of the true Gospel. Here is why it's so horrible. Because, this false movement will convert thousands to its ranks. It will grow like an out of control mustard tree. Many will partner with it thinking they are partnering with God, and thus it will turn millions into false converts. It will be a horrible time when some, who call themselves "Christians" or even a "friend" of Jesus, will indeed lead many astray creating more false converts like themselves.

But, before I move on I think you should know….

I think that time is now.

The Time is Now

The Quickly Approaching Rapture

On the planet over the last 100 years we have seen certain churches and groups that are teaching all of the things just covered. There are those that forbid some to marry in the name of religion, there are some who deny the true power of God and instead trade it for fake power and fake teaching. They are focused on pleasure and riches more than holiness and righteousness. They are all about speaking things into existence and treating God like He is a personal genie to supply their carnal needs. They teach crazy tales and lace exaggeration all throughout their teachings to bring about emotional responses. They incorporate music with false doctrine to bring people to a place of accepting their horrible phony gospel and teachings by bringing them into a happy state of euphoria. I think it's clear that there are a growing number of churches and teachers that bring a feel-good message and tell people what they want to hear in order to build their own kingdoms and bring in their own riches and pleasures.

Paul the Apostle, in 2 Thessalonians Chapter 2 told the believers that the Rapture wouldn't come *"except there come a falling away first"*. I don't think this is talking about true believers in Jesus Christ turning from the truth, but rather, an entire move that brings in a new form of false

The Quickly Approaching Rapture

Christianity based on pleasure and money rather than the true things of God. It will be supported by doctrines of demons and false signs and wonders. I also think this false church movement will incorporate different denominations and movements. Which, if you do a little research, this is happening right now, and I truly believe we are seeing the formation of a new one-world religion with these groups taking the lead. I also think this all lines up with the prophetic Laodicean church of Revelation. In the first line in His letter to that Church Jesus gives them the answer to their problem in His own personal description. It reads, ***"These things saith the Amen, the faithful and true witness, the beginning of the creation of God."*** (Rev 3:14). This fake church is based in lies and a false witness, but Jesus is the faithful and true witness. He then says this church thinks they are rich and in need of nothing but He says they are ***"wretched, and miserable, and poor, and blind, and naked."*** (Rev 3:17). He tells them to ***"anoint thine eyes with eye salve"*** because they are blind. They are blind to their own condition. They actually think they are Christians. They think they are correct and in need of nothing, but Jesus says they are blind. However, for them the door to Heaven is closed. Jesus is knocking on it (v.20),

The Quickly Approaching Rapture

which tells me it's almost time for Him to come for His Church. But He will leave behind the members of this fake last-days Church. In fact, we know in Matthew 7 how Jesus will answer them. It reads, *"<u>Not everyone that saith unto me, Lord, Lord,</u> shall enter into the kingdom of heaven; but he that doeth the will of my Father which is in heaven. <u>Many will say to me in that day, Lord, Lord, have we not prophesied in thy name? and in thy name have cast out devils? and in thy name done many wonderful works?</u> And then will I profess unto them, <u>I never knew you: depart from me, ye that work iniquity.</u>"* (Mat 7:21-23).

      As far as the order of things in 2 Thessalonians 2, I think Paul is saying that Jesus will not come until we see the great "falling away" and that just before the Rapture of the Church the Anti-Christ will appear on the world scene (2 Thes 2:3). But, the Anti-Christ is not going to take his position until the Holy Spirit is *"taken out of the way."* This does not mean the Holy Spirit will leave earth, as some teach, but I believe it simply means what it says. The Holy Spirit is restraining the Anti-Christ (v.7), but when He is simply moved out of the way, or in other words, gets out of the way of the advancement of the Anti-Christ at the appointed time, then this evil *"son of perdition"* (v.3) will rise to power.

Now, I have no problem thinking that the moving of the Holy Spirit out of the way of the advancement of the Anti-Christ could line up with the Rapture of the Church. In fact, that's the theory I lean to while writing this book. I believe that the taking of the Holy Spirit out of the way will indeed be timed with the Rapture of the Church. I don't know the day or the hour, obviously, but I do believe it's coming soon!

Context

Now that I have laid that all out I think it would be best to go back and read the entire passage. I think you will see a much clearer picture. 2 Thessalonians 2:1 starts, *"Now we beseech you, brethren, by the <u>coming of our Lord Jesus Christ</u>, and by our <u>gathering together</u> unto him, That ye be not soon shaken in mind, or be troubled, neither by spirit, nor by word, nor by letter as from us, as that <u>the day of Christ is at hand</u>. Let no man deceive you by any means: <u>for that day shall not come</u>, <u>except there come a falling away first</u>, and <u>that man of sin be revealed, the son of perdition;</u>"* Verse 6 continues, *"And now <u>you know what is restraining, that <u>he may be revealed in his</u></u>*

The Quickly Approaching Rapture

<u>own time</u>. For the mystery of lawlessness is already at work; only <u>He who now restrains will do so until He is taken out of the way</u>." (NKJ)

A side note on this passage that I want to make you aware of. Some say it proves that Jesus can't come at any moment because the "Apostasy" has to happen first. However, there has always been "Apostasy" in this world. From traitorous so-called believers in the early Church to false teaching and worldly religion that has grown all over the world since the third and fourth centuries, it has always been with us. And, it has included the entire description of evil practices written in Scripture. The "Apostasy" is all around us, and I don't think the Anti-Christ will be truly revealed until the Church is taken out. In these days I think it's just continued to get worse where it now seems very obvious. My guess is that every generation has thought they were in the "Apostasy" and that's what makes God's Word so amazing. He inspired it so that every generation would look for His coming with anticipation. This can most likely be said of many things in Scripture. It's just that we have the luxury of history and putting all things together, which sure seem to indicate the time is now!

Chapter 12

The Big Sign

Signs of the Times

Whenever I talk with individuals or groups about the "end times", or things of biblical prophecy and eschatology, people want to know how close we are and what the signs are that tell where we are on the prophetic timetable. I usually start with the standard answer, which is, that no man knows the day or the hour that the Lord will come for His Church (Mat 24:36). I also follow that up with verse 2 of 1 Thessalonians 5 where it states, *"For yourselves know perfectly that the day of the Lord so cometh as a thief in the night."*

In saying that, I usually follow that up with a reading of the passage just following the statement in 1 Thessalonians about the Lord coming like a thief in the night. I explain that this doesn't really apply to true believers. Verses 4-9 which read, *"But ye, brethren, are not in darkness, that that day should overtake you as a thief. Ye are all the children of light, and the children of*

The Quickly Approaching Rapture

<u>the day</u>: we are not of the night, <u>nor of darkness</u>. Therefore, let us not sleep, as do others; but let us <u>watch</u> and be sober. For they that sleep sleep in the night; and they that be drunken are drunken in the night. But let us, who are of the day, be sober, putting on the breastplate of faith and love, and for a helmet, the hope of salvation. For God <u>hath not appointed us to wrath</u>, but to obtain salvation by our Lord Jesus Christ."

Thief in the Night?

In this passage we see some key elements. First, at the end of the passage we see the reminder that we as believers are not appointed unto to wrath. I have already pointed out that the time of Tribulation is when God will indeed pour out His wrath on this world that rejected Him. Second, we see that Jesus is <u>not</u> coming like a ***"thief in the night"*** to those of us who love Him. Again, we don't know the day or the hour, but I truly believe this is telling us that we should be able to recognize the season leading up to His return. In other words, we should know when it's getting close. Jesus rebuked the Pharisees and Sadducees of His day, who didn't recognize the signs of His first coming (Mat 16:3, Luke 12:56). How much more then should we,

The Quickly Approaching Rapture

who are His, filled with His Spirit, be able to recognize the signs leading up to His imminent return for His Church?

Christmas Decorations

Anyone who has spent any time listening to Pastor Chuck Smith teach the Bible, particularly end times teachings, you already know the example I am going to use. But, even though many of us have heard it several times I still don't know a better story to illustrate what I am about to explain. Pastor Chuck loved to use an example about Christmas decorations. He would say that whenever you see the Christmas decorations being set up in the malls and stores around town it meant one thing—that Thanksgiving was right around the corner.

It's a funny statement, but he would then point out that if we are seeing signs around us of the Second Coming of Jesus Christ, then how much closer is our Thanksgiving? Better known as the Rapture of the Church.

Folks, the Rapture is soon. I don't know how soon. I don't know the day or the hour, but I know this, there are several signs pointing to the soon coming of Jesus Christ for His Church. Please, if your reading this book, and you don't know Jesus Christ as your personal Lord and Savior, now is the time. If you have never surrendered your life to Him. I beg you to do it now! He is coming soon!

"Nice story, you have any evidence?" You ask.

"Yes, but are you ready to see it?"

God's Billboard

In the book of Isaiah Chapter 11 we see an amazing prophetic Scripture. Verse 10-12 read, *"And in that day there shall be a <u>root of Jesse</u>, which shall stand for an <u>ensign of the people</u>; to it shall the <u>Gentiles seek</u>: and his rest shall be glorious. And it shall come to pass in that day, that the Lord shall set his hand again the second time to <u>recover the remnant of his people</u>, which shall be left, from Assyria, and from Egypt, and from Pathros, and from Cush, and from Elam, and from Shinar, and from Hamath, and from the islands of the sea. And <u>he shall set up an ensign for the nations</u>, and shall assemble the outcasts of Israel, and gather together the dispersed of Judah <u>from the four corners of the earth</u>."*

While this is a fairly long passage, there is so much in it that I felt I had to address it all.

The Quickly Approaching Rapture

First, this is clearly talking about Jesus as the *"Root of Jesse"*. Why? You ask. Simple, the "Root of Jesse" is talking about the line of Jesse, which is also the line of King David, which is also the line of the Messiah, Jesus Christ! So, when it says, *"in that day there shall be a root of Jesse"* it's talking about a day when the Messiah would come. We also know this with even more certainty because of the first four verses in Isaiah 11 which tell us that this *"Stem of Jesse"* (v.1) will bring with Him the *"Spirit of the Lord"* (v.2) and He will *"judge the poor and reprove with equity for the meek of the earth"* (v.4a). He will also, *"smite the earth with the rod of His mouth and with the breath of His lips He shall slay the wicked"* (v.4b).

In verse 10 of Isaiah 11 it tells us that this One, *"shall stand for an ensign of the people"*. The word there for *"ensign"* simply means a sign or signal. It then says one of the most amazing things ever, if you understand the Jewish culture and what this kind of statement would mean in that day. In Verse 10 it goes on to say, *"to it shall the Gentiles seek: and His rest shall be glorious."* This is pointing to Salvation of the Gentiles through the *"Root of Jesse"* Jesus Christ.

The Quickly Approaching Rapture

It then goes on to say that during this time of the Gentiles seeking Him that God will then *"recover the remnant of His people"* (v.11a). The Scripture explains that they were scattered, but God will bring them back. It goes on to say that God will then *"set up an ensign"* (a sign) *"for the nations"* when He assembles *"the outcasts of Israel and gather together the dispersed of Judah from the four corners of the earth."* (v.12).

On My 14, 1948 the nation of Israel was re-born. It had been decimated in the first century, and with the destruction of Jerusalem in 70 A.D. and the subsequent scattering of the Jews by brutal Roman leaders, the Jewish nation simply disappeared. The people of Israel then spread out among the nations and that's where they remained for nearly 1900 years. I find it fascinating that verse 12 in Isaiah 11 says that God will *"gather"* them from *"the four corners of the earth"* considering some of the world was still scarcely populated or uninhabited at the time of this prophecy and in 70 A.D.

In Isaiah chapter 66:8 we read, *"Who hath heard such a thing? who hath seen such things? Shall the earth be made to bring forth <u>in one day</u>? or shall a nation be*

The Quickly Approaching Rapture

<u>born at once</u>? for as soon as Zion travailed, she brought forth her children."

In Ezekiel 37 we see a story about a valley of dry bones. In the midst of that valley we see in verse 3 a question, *"And he said unto me, Son of man, can these bones live? And I answered, O Lord GOD, thou knowest."* In verses 4-5 it then states, *"Again he said unto me, Prophesy upon these bones, and say unto them, O ye dry bones, hear the word of the LORD. Thus, saith the Lord GOD unto these bones; Behold, I will cause breath to enter into you, and ye shall live."* In verse 12 we then read, *"Therefore, prophesy and say unto them, Thus saith the Lord GOD; Behold, O my people, I will open your graves, and cause you to come up out of your graves and bring you into the land of Israel."*

We also know that Israel had to become a nation to fulfill last days prophecy because the city of Jerusalem is its capitol. In the book of Zechariah Chapter 12:2-3 we read that Jerusalem will indeed be restored in the last days and the whole world would be focused on this tiny country and this small city. It reads, *"Behold, <u>I will make Jerusalem a cup of trembling unto all the people round about</u>, when they shall be in the siege both against Judah and against*

The Quickly Approaching Rapture

Jerusalem. And <u>in that day</u> will <u>I make Jerusalem a burdensome stone for all people</u>: all that burden themselves with it shall be cut in pieces, though all the people of the earth be gathered together against it."

We know there is a day coming when the world will come against Israel and Jerusalem, but that day isn't yet. However, think about how much news this one nation and this one city seem to be a part of. When the United States moved their embassy to Jerusalem how much of a stir did that cause? How much talk is there in the world about this place? It seems to me it's a lot more than most places, and I believe that's only going to increase.

"Okay, so Israel is a nation again, how does that impact us today, and how is that a "big sign", You ask.

Simple, the first thing is that the very re-birth of the nation was prophesied thousands of years before it happened, and this is a really big deal because no nation has ever done anything like this ever. Do you know that the Jewish people kept their identity and brought back the mostly dead language of Hebrew after 1900 years? Think about that. For nearly 19 centuries an entire people kept their identity and have done exactly what the Bible

The Quickly Approaching Rapture

predicted. They subsequently went home to the Land God gave them from all over the globe. Israel now has the largest population of Jewish people in the world, more than any other one nation. Think about it, in one day they became a nation again, after 1900 years! Not only that, but Jerusalem is now a burden for many in the world, just as the Bible predicted.

For many of the last days prophecies to occur Israel had to be a nation again. This is where something like "replacement theology" got its birth. When Israel was still not re-born (Prior to 1948) some in the Christian Church decided to "help God out". That never works out well just so you know. I mean ask Abraham and Sarah. In any case, they decided to start placing all the promises given to Israel on the Church. I guess they forgot the entire Chapter of Romans 11, but I am not going to dive into that here. However, what I am going to say is that for many of the prophecies predicted in Scripture to occur, such as the, "Time of Jacob's Trouble" (Dan 9, Jer 30), or the 144,000 Jewish witnesses from 12 Tribes of Israel in Revelation Chapter 7, or the two witnesses of Revelation 11, or the war prophesied in Ezekiel 38, or even the battle of Armageddon in Revelation 16, for any of these to happen in the last days, Israel had to be a nation once again—and they are! This is the biggest sign that we are in the last of the last days.

Chapter 13

More Signs of the Times

In the News

Before we dive into this Chapter I want to put out a word of caution. We need to be careful that we don't try to apply every news story, event, tragedy, natural disaster or even a pandemic, as something specifically mentioned in Scripture. What I mean by this is that if something like a large earthquake happens or something like the Covid-19 event occurs, we shouldn't pull out a single verse and say, "see here it is!" Now, don't get me wrong there are some events that will transpire that will have verses that apply to them. I can think of no bigger even than that of the Rapture of the Church, but I just want us to be careful.

When I look at news stories that seem to have biblical relevance I look for patterns. The reason I do this is because I think that's how Jesus said we would understand the times in which we live. In Luke 21 He told His disciples that *"many shall come in my name"* but to not be *"deceived"* (v.8). He went on to describe things that will happen in the last days, *"But when ye shall hear of <u>wars and commotions</u>, be not terrified: for these things must*

The Quickly Approaching Rapture

first come to pass; but the end is not by and by. Then said he unto them, Nation shall rise against nation, and kingdom against kingdom: And <u>great earthquakes</u> shall be in divers places, and <u>famines</u>, and <u>pestilences</u>; and <u>fearful sights and great signs shall there be from heaven.</u>" (v.9-11). He also told His disciples that before any of these things just listed will happen, that they themselves would be persecuted, which did occur.

Pestilence: World-Wide Pandemics

When we look at that word *"pestilences"* in verse 11 we see that it is the Greek word "Loimos". According to *Strong's* it means "a plague". So, when we see things like the world-wide Covid event we know that this is just one of the "pestilences" that will occur and have occurred. However, the thing that makes this newest pestilence different is global communication and instant news has escalated the fear and the reactions to it. It's not to say it's not as serious as others, it's really too early to know that, but it's certainly hitting the world in a way that no pandemic has ever done in the modern era. And, it's just one event in the latest of a string of such events, that modern medicine and science at one-time thought would no longer trouble mankind. From Aids, to Ebola, to SARS, to Zika, to the West Nile, to Swine Flu and Bird Flu, the modern world is experiencing epidemics and pandemics even with all of our modern medical advancements. While

The Quickly Approaching Rapture

many of the previous examples were fairly recent there have been many more in history. One from the last century is one I doubt any of you would remember. The influenza pandemic known as the "Spanish Flu" in 1918 killed as many as 500 million people in a two-year span. Imagine if something so deadly, that wasn't treatable, hit the world today with nearly 8 billion people alive. What would be the outcome?

Earthquakes, Famines, Great Signs from Heaven

The Bible states in Luke 21:11 that *"great earthquakes shall be in diverse places"*. It also says that *"famines"* will occur and *"fearful sights"* and *"great signs shall there be from heaven"* in the days leading up to His return for His Church.

First, *"great earthquakes"*.

Has there been a pattern of increasing "great" earthquakes? I honestly don't know. From some sources they say yes, from others they say no. I wasn't able to get a clear answer so I want to be responsible with the topic. What I do know however, is that with modern media technology we hear about them more. I also see that there are earthquakes in places that don't usually have them, and some particularly bad earthquakes that have caused some horrible disasters. Earthquakes like the one in Haiti in 2010

The Quickly Approaching Rapture

that is estimated to have killed over 300,000 people. Or, the 2011 earthquake in Japan that caused the nuclear disaster at Fukushima. In 2004 a 9.1 earthquake hit the Indian Ocean causing nearly a quarter-of-million deaths and devastation that was just not imaginable at the time. Iran, Kashmir, China, they have all had deadly earthquakes in recent years.

However,…

Don't you love when I say that?

I don't see where the Bible says that earthquakes will increase…. Only that they will be in "diverse" places. In fact, I do not see anywhere in the Bible where pestilences or famines will increase either. Only that they will be part of the last days in diverse places. Which lines up with what Jesus said in Matthew 24:7, *"and there shall be famines, and pestilences, and earthquakes, in divers places."*

Jesus own words tell us that all of these things will happen in *"divers"* places not necessarily that they will increase. Anyone who has been around a while and pays attention knows that all of things are part of our world.

The Quickly Approaching Rapture

Even with all the modern advancements there are still episodes of famine, and we can't stop earthquakes, and these are certainly happing in diverse places, and we know about the pestilences. We also know that there have been wars all over the globe, especially the last 100 years. But what about the "great signs from heaven?"

Strange Weather

What I have seen increase in recent years is strange weather patterns that can't be easily explained away.

Before I start down this road I also want to make sure you understand that what I am about to tell you is <u>my own opinion</u> of things, and <u>my own theory</u> of what is happening. I share this with you only because I have developed this theory over years and I have tried to make sure that anything I look at concerning prophetic events I do with Scripture as my test. I am not saying my theory is 100 percent Bible accurate, and I am not saying it is exactly what is going to occur. What I am saying is that there does seem to be some physical evidence aligned with biblical evidence that could mean certain things are coming.

Back to the weather. So, have you all noticed the crazy weather patterns the last decade or so? While many in society call things like this "global warming" or "global climate change" I call it *"fearful sights"* which is what Luke 21:11 states, *"great signs shall there be from heaven".*

One of the remarkable signs I have seen growing is the number of floods and heavy rainstorms hitting the globe. The Guardian website published an article that pointed out that flooding around the planet has increased upwards of 50 percent over a decade. The article explains that this is up "four times higher than in 1980".[xvii]

And, while you wouldn't think the two could exist together, another thing that seems to be getting much worse are wildfires. According to the Insurance Information Institute's website[xviii], the United States alone has seen a dramatic increase in wildfires since the year 2000. There have been a handful of moderate years mixed in, according to their chart, but when you look at the data it's obvious. Wildfires are getting worse. If you go do your own research on this topic you will see it's alarming. Something is definitely going on, and if you ask most people they simply say that it's climate change or global warming. These same people usually then attribute climate change to the actions of people.

The Quickly Approaching Rapture

The thing is… they are right.

Let me explain….

The Sky Is Falling

The Bible says that during the Tribulation many horrible events will occur. We know that there will be war, famine and pestilence like never seen before in human history. But we also know some pretty scary and horrifying things are going to happen beyond that. There are going to be things hitting the earth causing tremendous damage. So much damage that Revelation 8:12 tells us that the light of the sun and the moon will be diminish greatly. We also know that in Revelation 8:7 we see that a third of the trees and all the grass of the earth is burned up by something described as *"hail and fire"*. We know that Revelation 8:8 says something like a *"great mountain burning with fire"* will hit the sea and a third of the sea will become *"blood"* which will kill a third of the fish and creatures of the sea and destroy a third of the ships in the sea (v.9). We then see in Revelation 8:10 that another *"great star"* falls *"burning as it were a lamp"* and upon a third of the *"rivers"* and *"fountains of waters"*. This star is called *"Wormwood"* and it causes a third of the waters to become *"bitter"* (v.11). Which, brings us to verse 12 again which states that

The Quickly Approaching Rapture

a third of the light of the sun and moon will be *"smitten"*. Then in verse 13 we see that an angel gives a warning about what is yet to come. Meaning, it's about to get worse.

Joshua Again

I want to pause here and give some back story to my theory. Again, my theory is based on what is currently happening to our planet comparing it to evidence in the Scripture and trying to understand what it might be pointing to. One of the most fascinating things that I found in my study of Scripture is in the book of Joshua. I already shared with you the beautiful picture of Christ in that book, but now let me share with you something I found that may or may not be related to what is happening now and will happen on planet Earth during the Tribulation.

In Joshua Chapter 10 we see an interesting story about a king of Jerusalem named Adonizedec (v.1). He had heard about Joshua taking the city of Ai, and how Joshua had made peace with the Gibeonites, who were a mighty people. So, this king mustered up a coalition of four other kings and decided to go to battle with the Gibeonites. Joshua is given word about this and comes to the defense of the Gibeonites. Israel and the Gibeonites had victory, but the armies of the Amorites were fleeing from Joshua's

The Quickly Approaching Rapture

army and getting away. In Joshua 10:11 we see that as these armies were fleeing they were hit with *"great stones form heaven"*. Then in verse 12 we see Joshua asking the Lord to literally stop the sun in the sky so his armies could finish off their enemy. Verse 13 reads, *"And the <u>sun stood still, and the moon stayed</u>, until the people had avenged themselves upon their enemies. Is not this written in the book of Jasher? So, the sun stood still in the midst of heaven, and hasted not to go down <u>about a whole day</u>."*

This is quite remarkable when you think about it. God stopped the earth from rotating somehow to make the sun and moon appear to stand still for *"about a whole day"* so that Israel could have daylight to finish off their enemies. Talk about daylight savings time!

"Cool story, but what does this have to do with the end times?" You ask with a tiny bit of impatience.

Well, again, <u>it's only a theory</u>, but what caused the earth to stand still? Could there have been something so massive, so large, within just the perfect gravitational pull, that it could have caused the earth to slow its rotation? Also, I find it curious that a bunch of stones from heaven fell on the armies before the earth stood still. When I compare that to Revelation Chapter 8 I also see that *"hail and fire"* (v.7) fall on the Earth just before a *"great mountain burning with fire"* (v.8) hits the seas of the Earth. Then in Verse 10 another *"great star"* named *"Wormwood"* hits the planet causing even more horrible damage. Now, some claim these things being described in Revelation 8 are nuclear bombs, etc. I guess that's as good a theory as mine, but I also know if there were something large in our solar system, large enough, with a returning orbit close to our planet, it could cause a debris field to hit our earth and cause tremendous damage. It also seems to me that if such a large object were present, it could cause the earth to start to do weird things like earthquakes, floods, strange weather patterns, pole shifting or moving, and if larger objects within that debris field hit the earth, it would certainly knock our earth out of its current position, rotation and orbit, and cause it to stagger.

Sound far-fetched? Well, the Bible says that during the Tribulation events like this will occur. First, back in Luke 21 verse 25 we read, *"And there shall be signs in the sun, and in the moon, and in the stars; and upon the earth distress of nations, with perplexity; the sea and the waves roaring."* Jesus then adds, *"Men's hearts failing them for fear, and for looking after those things which are coming on the earth: for the powers of heaven shall be shaken"* (v.26).

When I look at verse 26 of Luke 21 I see that whatever is coming *"on"* the planet is going to cause *"men's hearts"* to fail. That doesn't seem like a small thing. It seems like "the end of the world" type of thing.

In Isaiah Chapter 24 I believe the Bible is speaking about the same events as the passages in Luke and Revelation. In verse 20 it reads, *"The earth shall reel to and fro like a drunkard and shall be removed like a cottage; and the transgression thereof shall be heavy upon it; and it shall fall, and not rise again."* We know this is speaking of the time of the end because of Verse 21, *"And it shall come to pass in that day, that the LORD shall punish the host of the high ones that are on high, and the kings of the earth upon the earth."* Verse 23 also states, *"Then the moon shall be confounded, and the sun ashamed, when the LORD of hosts shall reign in mount Zion, and in Jerusalem, and before his ancients gloriously."*

The Quickly Approaching Rapture

Over the years I have heard many Christian theologians and those who study Creation and the Flood of Noah, describe to me that a meteor or comet or some large object most likely triggered the Great Flood. I don't know if that's true for sure, but I have seen some pretty good evidence. Modern secular science even believes that the dinosaurs were killed off by a meteor or comet, etc. We as Christians know the real timing of that, but that's another book for another day. Still, I find it interesting that in 2 Peter Chapter 3 we see that in the last days people are even going to deny the flood. Verses 3-4 states, *"Knowing this first, that there shall come in the last days scoffers, walking after their own lusts, And saying, Where is the promise of his coming? for since the fathers fell asleep, all things continue as they were from the beginning of the creation."* Verses 5-6 then continues, *" For this they willingly are ignorant of, that by the word of God the heavens were of old, and the earth standing out of the water and in the water: Whereby the world that then was, being overflowed with water, perished."* It then switches to a last days judgement warning in Verse 7, *"But the heavens and the earth, which are now, by the same word*

The Quickly Approaching Rapture

are kept in store, reserved unto fire against the day of judgment and perdition of ungodly men."

So, in the last days there will be scoffers who won't even recognize the judgment of the flood. Think about any science class you took in secular schools or institutions. They do not believe in a global flood!

But, the passage goes on to say that these same deniers will be those that go after their own *"lusts"*. But, verse 7 says that *"But the <u>heavens</u> and the <u>earth</u>, which are now, by the same word are kept in store"* God inspires the author to then point out that *"by the same word are kept in store, reserved unto fire against the day of judgment and perdition of ungodly men."* Whatever is being *"kept in store"* is *"reserved"* by God until that *"fire"* and *"day of judgement"*.

My theory is simply that whatever caused the Earth to stand still during Joshua's day, brought with it some kind of large stones hitting the earth. I look at Revelation, and the similarity of what is going to happen in the Tribulation, and it's easy to see something will hit the planet. In fact, hail and fire, followed by a great mountain, followed by star called Wormwood. All three going to hit this planet and cause horrible damage. I also know it will cause the

The Quickly Approaching Rapture

Earth to stagger like a drunk man and whatever is coming upon the Earth will cause men's hearts to fail them. It sounds horrible, and I don't want to be here for it!
Boom!
Going back to the increased flooding, diverse earthquakes, and increased wildfires. Here is what I think, take it or leave it. <u>Again, just my theory and opinion, nothing more.</u> But, I think something is pulling on the planet and causing strange weather patterns, the magnetic poles to move, climates in different regions to change, and even strange booms and sounds like the creaking of an old house sitting on a shifting landscape.

Oh wait...

You haven't heard about those strange noises?

Loud booms and the like?

Go Google "strange booms heard around the world" and then look at all the news stories on television and published on several news websites about such booms. They are happening everywhere, but no one seems to know what they are or why they are happening.

Again, I think something big is pulling on the planet, and I think the impact of such a gravitational force could be instrumental in what is going on now with the

The Quickly Approaching Rapture

noises, earthquakes, magnetic poles and strange weather patterns.

Evidence

As far as hard evidence, I don't know that I have that. But, again, this is just simply my theory. However, I have seen several articles on television broadcasts, in newspapers and on various websites recently that the Earth's magnetic pole keep shifting for some unknown reason. Even Business Insider posted an article on their website titled, "Earth's magnetic north pole is skittering wildly across the Arctic. By 2040, our compasses 'will point eastward of true North,' an expert says."[xix] I don't know if you think this is odd or not, but personally, this doesn't sound normal to me.

I have also seen news articles from decades ago about a "tenth planet" being possible. Well, I guess now that Pluto has been demoted, it would technically be a ninth planet. But if you go back and do the research over the last fifty years or so, there have been various theories about another planet, or something large in our solar system that we just can't confirm. In fact, even a recent mathematical discovery seems to back this up. On NASA's Solar System website there is a story relating to this "Hypothetical Planet

The Quickly Approaching Rapture

X".[xx] The site indicates that "mathematical evidence" does suggest that Planet X may exist, but before I go too far, I am not saying <u>this</u> is what will hit our planet during the Tribulation. It could be pushing or pulling a debris field with it that may have objects that do so, or another object or object(s) all together could be the answer. What I am saying is that the simple fact that this possible planet, or at the very least, a mathematical anomaly, was just officially discovered recently, should make you realize that man is not as smart as we think we are, and there are things still out there we don't know about. I also know that when the Bible says that things are going to hit our planet, it means just that. Something is coming. We know that multiple objects are going to hit our planet during the Tribulation, and what I know is that they have to come from somewhere. If they are what I have suggested, then they are currently on their way and there is no way to stop them.

    "Okay, nice theory, but you said <u>we</u> caused it. How is that even possible?" You say with frustration.

    "Hold on, let me explain."

    You see, people are the cause of the climate change that is here and the drastic climate change of the

The Quickly Approaching Rapture

Tribulation. But, it may not be caused by what we drive, what we burn, or what, and how much we consume. When mankind fell in the Garden of Eden, it set in motion tragic events. The S-I-N Virus pandemic began. It has since spread to every human being that has ever lived, and the statistical data shows that 100% of all human beings are infected with it, and all will die physically because of it.

When we look at all that has come upon this planet we have no one to blame but ourselves. Sin has a real impact on the physical world. Think of the sin of Adam, but then think of our collective sin as human beings over the centuries. Think about every sin happening at this very moment among the nearly 8 billion people on the planet. Sin is the cause of every "natural disaster" horrible event, pandemic, war, flood, etc. Sin is the cause. It all has an impact on this world, and because of it, God's wrath and judgment has to come. Why? You ask. Because God is Perfect and Holy and Just. He must judge sin because He's a Perfect Judge. But, He is also a loving God and He provided a way for you and me to escape His Wrath, His Judgment, the Tribulation, and an eternity separated from Him in a real place called Hell.

The Quickly Approaching Rapture

Imagine if the media, world governments, and every individual, would react to the disease of sin the way they do with a viral pandemic. Every human being since Adam has been infected. This is why Jesus Christ, through the mystery of the Incarnation, became a man. He was fully man and fully God. It's called the Hypostatic Union, and it's something that scholars and critics have been trying to understand or undermine since His death, burial, Resurrection and Ascension. But, as I often say, if you have a God so small you can figure him out then why would you worship him? I know my God is amazing, and no one understands Him completely. But this same infinitely dimensional God loves us so much that He paid our price.

The Bible says in John 3:16 that God so loved the world that He sent His One and Only Son, Jesus, that whoever would believe in Him would not perish but have eternal life! John 3:17 states that God didn't send His Son into the world to condemn it, but *"that the world through Him might be saved"*.

I wonder, do you understand what that means?

The Quickly Approaching Rapture

For those of you that do, what a wonderful God we serve. You and I will not have to endure the Tribulation, His Wrath, His Judgment, or Hell. We will spend eternity with Him!

But, for those of you who don't know Him, now is the time to surrender. The wrath of God is coming, and whatever is going to hit our planet is going to hit it. Whatever is coming upon this planet is going to cause men's hearts to fail. That sounds like something so fearful, so intense, so horrible, that no one in their right mind would want to endure it. If you don't know Jesus Christ as your Lord and Savior, the time is now. Don't wait. You may not have another opportunity. The men and women of Noah's day didn't heed the warning. Do not make the same mistake they did!

Chapter 14

The Quickly Approaching Rapture

Where is Our Hope?

In the book of Titus Chapter 2 we see the Rapture described in two simple, but profound words, *"Blessed Hope"* (v.13). It's part of an amazing chapter, but three verses stand out to me. Titus 2:11-13 reads, *"For the grace of God that bringeth salvation hath appeared to all men, Teaching us that, <u>denying ungodliness and worldly lusts</u>, we should live soberly, righteously, and godly, in this present world; Looking for that <u>blessed hope</u>, and the <u>glorious appearing</u> of the <u>great God</u> and our Saviour Jesus Christ."*

First, this passage reminds us in the last part of verse 13 that Jesus Christ is indeed God. He is described as "the great God and Savior". What a comfort in trying times.

Second, the very first statement in verse 11 reminds us that we are saved by Grace alone (Eph 2:8), and as the verse continues we are reminded of the remedy to the "apostasy" of these last days (*"denying ungodliness and worldly lusts).*

The passage then goes on to remind us that we, as Christians, indeed have a *"blessed hope"* and it comes in the form of *"the glorious appearing of the great God and Savior Jesus Christ."*

The Rapture, for the true Christian, is a *"blessed hope"*. It's the very thing we are all waiting for. In this book I have laid out several things in regard to the Rapture of the Church, and in this Chapter I hope to bring it all together. I pray I can do it justice.

The Foundation

The foundation of our "Blessed Hope" is the promise that Jesus gave us. He said, *"I go to prepare a place for you"* (John 14:2b). He then states in verse 3, *"And if I go and prepare a place for you, I will come again, and receive you unto myself; that where I am, there ye may be also."*

This promise Jesus made will be kept. As I mentioned earlier in this book, while God can do so many things that we are not able to number them, there are actually things God can't do. He can't learn, because He

The Quickly Approaching Rapture

knows all, He can't lie because He is Truth, and another thing He can't do is break a promise!

If Jesus said He will come again for us to take us where He is, a place He prepared for us, then you can bank on it. But know this, He also tells us that He is coming for a faithful Church that held to His Word and didn't deny His Name (Rev 3). Also know, that although the Rapture is quickly approaching, there are many who claim to be believers in Jesus Christ who will be left behind.

How Soon?

I have already told you my frequent answer about not knowing the day or hour. But, I also follow that up with a comment that requires a grin. I usually tell people who ask me to give a timeline of when Jesus will return for His Church, that, "If He doesn't come today, He will be here tomorrow, and that's true every day!" Think about it…

I then explain that while my comment is lighthearted, it is also how we are supposed to live. We are to live as if Jesus is coming for us at any moment, because, that's exactly what the Scripture says about His coming. It could come at any moment. This is called "the imminent return of Jesus Christ" and it's clearly displayed in Scripture.

The Quickly Approaching Rapture

I also point to Matthew 24, Luke 21 and Mark 13 as Chapters in the Bible that tell us the soon return of our Lord could be right around the corner. As we read the headlines in the News, or witness the events around us, it is clear—the time for our Lord's Return is quickly approaching.

Signs the Rapture is Near

In Mark 13 Jesus is with His disciples. They have just come out of the Temple and are having a conversation. The disciples mention how wonderful the Temple is, to which, Jesus replies(v.2), *"Seest thou these great buildings? there shall not be left one stone upon another, that shall not be thrown down."* Then Peter, James and John take Jesus aside and ask Him two questions, *"Tell us, when shall these things be? and what shall be the sign when all these things shall be fulfilled?"* (v.4). In other words, they wanted Jesus to explain when the Temple would be destroyed, and further, when the culmination of all things would be.

Jesus starts by warning them not to be deceived (v.5). He goes on to tell them that many are going to come in His name claiming to be Christ and those same people would deceive many (v.6). Jesus then describes the fact that they will hear of wars and rumors of wars, but Jesus tells

The Quickly Approaching Rapture

them that they shouldn't worry because these things must come to pass. Jesus then also states, *"but the end shall not be yet"* (v.7). He adds in verse 8, *"For nation shall rise against nation, and kingdom against kingdom: and there shall be earthquakes in divers places, and there shall be famines and troubles: these are the beginnings of sorrows."* In Luke 21 Verse 11, of this same conversation, we read, *"And great earthquakes shall be in divers places, and famines, and pestilences; and fearful sights and great signs shall there be from heaven."* In Matthew 24:7-8 we get some additional information from Jesus, *"For nation shall rise against nation, and kingdom against kingdom: and there shall be famines, and pestilences, and earthquakes, in divers places. <u>All these are the beginning of sorrows</u>."*

Birth Pangs

In other words, Jesus says when we <u>start to see</u> *"great earthquakes"* in *"divers places"* and *"famines"* and *"pestilences"* and *"fearful sights and great signs"* that these are just the *"beginning of sorrows"*. In the NASB translation of the Holy Bible this is described as *"birth pangs"* and I find the term revealing. Jesus explains to His disciples in Verse 8 that many of the signs He just

The Quickly Approaching Rapture

explained are merely *"birth pangs"* and in essence, they will continue to get worse and closer together as the Rapture approaches. I think this is a great analogy because when we are talking about the return of Christ, while we don't know the exact timing, we know that the world is pregnant with anticipation. We may not know exactly when the baby is due, but we can certainly see that the belly is growing, and it's only a matter of time. Remember in 1 Thessalonians Chapter 5 Verse 4 we are told that true believers in Jesus Christ will not be surprised by the Rapture, *"But ye, brethren, are not in darkness, that that day should overtake you as a thief."*

Also, in Hebrews 10 we see an encouragement for believers to continue to live godly and to continue to gather together *"so much the more, as ye see the day approaching"* (v.25).

In Luke 21 Jesus gives us a better understanding of the timing of the Rapture. After describing the events that are going to occur in Israel soon, and the events in the last days just before His return, He then says, *"And when these things <u>begin to come to pass</u>, then look up, and lift up your heads; for your redemption draweth nigh"* (v.28).

The Quickly Approaching Rapture

In this verse Jesus is saying when the previously stated earthquakes, famines, pestilences, and great signs *"begin"* to happen, then look up because the timing is near for His return!

I ask you; have we begin to see these things?

The Last Generation

Not only that, but in 2 Timothy Chapter 3 we see the description of what the generation would look like in the days leading up to the Rapture. In Verses 1-7 we read, *"This know also, that in the last days perilous times shall come. ² For men shall <u>be lovers of their own selves</u>, covetous, boasters, proud, blasphemers, disobedient to parents, unthankful, unholy, ³ Without natural affection, trucebreakers, false accusers, incontinent, fierce, despisers of those that are good, ⁴ Traitors, heady, highminded, lovers of pleasures more than lovers of God; ⁵ Having a form of godliness, but denying the power thereof: from such turn away."*

When you look at this description it sure seems to sound like the days we live.

Verse 1: *"Perilous times"*

The Quickly Approaching Rapture

Verse 2: People are going to be *"lovers of their own selves"* We are the generation that invented the selfie for Pete's sake!

Verse 2: It continues to explain people are going to be *"covetous, boasters, proud, blasphemers, disobedient to parents, unthankful, unholy."* I ask you again, doesn't this sound like our current generation?

Verse 3: *"Without natural affection"* Just consider abortion, in which, a mother can kill their own child in her own womb! Or, think about the modern dating scene with apps that are created for a quick "hook up" with no strings attached.

The passage goes on to say people won't keep their word, they will be *"false accusers"* and that they will despise those who are good. Have you seen our modern political situation? Do you see how Christians are being treated around the globe?

Verse 4: *"Traitors"* will arise along with those that think way too highly of themselves and love pleasure more than God.

Verse 5: We see it's related to verse 4 in that, these who love pleasure more than God also have a *"form of godliness"* but they deny the true *"power"* of God.

The Quickly Approaching Rapture

Apostasy Growing

As mentioned in Chapter 11 of this book, we are currently seeing things that appear to be lined up with a last days "Apostasy". Verses 4 and 5 of 2 Timothy Chapter 3 are certainly describing that. Which, in itself is a huge sign the Return of Christ is near! After all, we have seen this verse quite a bit in this book, but it bears repeating, ***"Let no man deceive you by any means: for that day shall not come, except there come a falling away first"*** (2 Thes 2:3).

Again, that word for *"falling away"* is "Apostasia" in Greek and "Apostasy" in English. As discussed, a very good case can be made that we are currently in this time of "Apostasy". This "Apostasy" is a movement that is selfish, self-centered, based in experience over obedience, and natural over spiritual. It includes those who deny the power of God by settling for fake signs and miracles and they make God their puppet or genie by claiming they can speak things into existence. These are those that morph into a form of godliness for the sake of show and put on their godly costumes. They preach a gospel that is anything but good news. They preach a gospel based in material things and not based in the Word of God. This "Apostasy" isn't just one group or denomination either. We also see that there are some among this last days falling away that also forbid some to marry and "abstain" from meats. As previously noted, these seem to be harsh religious rules that would be dictated to those who follow this doctrine. All of these who are part of this "Apostasy" will be left behind, and most likely, most of them will be part of the one-world religion of the Tribulation under the leadership of a powerful and famous religious leader that will no doubt be connected to Christianity. After all, we read in Revelation 13:11 that this false religious leader, who will aid the Anti-Christ, will have the horns of a *"lamb"* but speak like a *"dragon"*. I believe the *"lamb"* reference is displaying his false Christianity and his words like a *"dragon"* display his demonic motivation.

Instant World-Wide Communication

Another sign that we are very close to the return of Christ for His Church can be found in Revelation 11. In this Chapter of the Bible we see that God is going to send Two Witnesses during the Tribulation to prophesy for three-and-a-half years (v.3). If you study this out you will see that these witnesses are going to perform the same miracles that Moses and Elijah did while on Earth. I am not going to look deeper at this in this book, but some think the two

The Quickly Approaching Rapture

witnesses will, in fact, be Moses and Elijah, while others have different theories. For the sake of this study we are only looking at what happens to these witnesses. They preach in Jerusalem and against the evil of this world. It says that through the signs they bring, it will *"torment them that dwelt on the earth"* (v.10).

In verse 7 of Revelation 11 we see that once these Two Witnesses have *"finished their testimony"* the *"beast"* will then be given the power by God to kill them. Again, not until God says they are done does this happen. God will be in complete control even if the beast and others don't think so. Nevertheless, the beast kills them, and what do we see? We see the fact that their bodies will lay dead in the streets of Jerusalem and the whole world will see it happen (v.8). Not only that, but it says in Revelation 11:10 that the people of the world will rejoice and send gifts to each other.

"So what?" You might ask.

"Well, do you realize when this was being written? This was first century."

"Okay, and...?" You ask.

The Quickly Approaching Rapture

Simply this, how would the first century, or any century until the twentieth century, have been able to see Jerusalem from all around the globe? Before satellite television, smartphones and the internet, we couldn't see a live feed of Jerusalem. Not only that, but until nearly the same time-period we were not able to send gifts to one another around the world. With the advancement in postal services, package delivery, Amazon and the like, we can now do what verse 10 states and send gifts all over the globe to each other.

In Revelation 11:11 we see that God will then resurrect these Two Witnesses after three-and-a-half days and in verse 12 it says, *"their enemies beheld them"*. In other words, the enemies of God saw this happen. At this same time verse 13 says a *"great earthquake"* will hit Jerusalem. You have to believe the enemies of God will be trembling, and it won't be from the ground shaking.

Knowledge and Technology

In the days leading up to the Day of the Lord (Tribulation) the Bible also says that knowledge will increase. In Daniel Chapter 12 Verse 4 we read, *"But thou, O Daniel, shut up the words, and seal the book, even to*

The Quickly Approaching Rapture

the time of the end: many shall run to and fro, and knowledge shall be increased."

We have certainly seen an increase in knowledge over the last 100 years, and it continues to grow rapidly. Another passage in Nahum concerning the last days also seems to point to the creation of some kind of transportation that will be like nothing before it. Nahum 2:3-4 it says that *"in the day of his preparation"* (v.3) that ***"chariots shall rage in the streets, they shall justle one against another in the broad ways: they shall seem like torches, they shall run like the lightnings"*** (v.4). Does this not sound like modern automobiles and streets and highways?

The Big Sign

In Chapter 12 we looked at the biggest sign that we are living in the last days. That sign is Israel. We know that in the very last days Israel will become a nation again, and that it would become a world focus. This is obvious when reading the various passages throughout Scripture. In Zechariah 12:2-3 we read, ***"Behold, I will make Jerusalem a cup of trembling unto all the people round about, when they shall be in the siege both against Judah and against Jerusalem. And in that day will I make Jerusalem a***

The Quickly Approaching Rapture

burdensome stone for all people: all that burden themselves with it shall be cut in pieces, though all the people of the earth be gathered together against it."

All through the book of Revelation we see evidence of this as well. Whether it's the 144,000 Jewish men from 12 Tribes of Israel, the Two Witnesses testifying in Jerusalem itself, or even the Battle of Armageddon, all of it happens within the boundaries of Israel.

When Israel became a nation again in 1948 it should have been an alarm for the world to wake up! Jesus Christ is coming for His Church, and the time of the Tribulation is right around the corner. After all, the Tribulation itself is known as "The Time of Jacob's Trouble", which is seven years that God has yet to complete with His Nation Israel according to the prophecy of Daniel.

Which View is Best?

When looking at the various views of the Rapture, the Post, Mid, Pre-Wrath, and Pre-Tribulation viewpoints, I hope that you have been able to see why I personally hold to the latter. The Pre-Tribulation Rapture accounts for all of the elements of the Rapture, it's purpose, it's promise and it's timing.

The Quickly Approaching Rapture

Post Problems In My Opinion

The Post-Tribulation viewpoint, which believes that Christ will come at the end of the Tribulation for His Church, must account for the fact that God is going to be pouring out His Wrath on the world during that time-period. The problem is that the Scripture clearly states believers are not appointed unto His Wrath (1 Thes 5:9).

Also, they must account for the seven-years that are still appointed to the nation of Israel to fulfill God's promise (Dan 9). They must also account for the promise that Jesus made to believers that He was going to prepare a place for them, and that, He would come again and take believers to that place (John 14). If this is at the end of the Tribulation, and we know from Revelation 19 and Zechariah 14, that Jesus is going to physically return to this planet at His Second Coming, then how would that make sense? We get taken up to immediately be brought back to Earth. For what purpose? Where is the place He prepared for us?

Not only that, but in Titus we read that the Rapture is every believers *"blessed hope"*. How is it that our *"blessed hope"* if we have to endure God's Wrath for seven years?

The Quickly Approaching Rapture

Also, the Bible is clear. We should expect the imminent Return of Jesus Christ. Meaning, He could come at any moment. In Luke 12:40 Jesus states, *"Be ye therefore ready also: for the Son of man cometh at an hour when ye think not."* Which begs the question, how could He come when *"ye think not"* if the Tribulation and all its events are happening?

Mid and Pre-Wrath Problems In My Opinion

The Mid-Tribulation and Pre-Wrath theories have some of the same issues as the Post-Tribulation theory. The biggest one is the seven years allotted to Israel to bring about God's promise. If those seven years are something set aside for Israel (Dan 9), and in Romans 11 we read that Israel was blinded, in part, until the fullness of the Gentiles comes in, then why would God allow the Church to go through part of this seven-year time-period allotted to the Jewish nation and saturated with His wrath?

Also, in the first set of plagues in Revelation 6 we see that the *"Great Day of His Wrath is come; and who shall be able to stand?"* (v.17). If we as believers are not appointed unto wrath, how can we be present for this?

The Quickly Approaching Rapture

No Rapture

For those who do not believe in a Rapture of the Church my hope is that you have seen enough evidence to change your mind. The Bible clearly teaches the doctrine of the Rapture, and if you still can't see it, my hope is that you will prayerfully consider your rejection.

Preterism

For those who hold to Preterism, in that, they believe that all or most of the events described in Mark 13, Luke 21, and Matthew 24 already happened in 70 A.D. with the destruction of Jerusalem and the Temple, I suggest you go back and read Jesus' comments about the time of Tribulation coming upon the whole world. In fact, let me place those here.

In Mark 13:19 Jesus says, *"For in those days shall be affliction, <u>such as was not from the beginning of the creation which God created unto this time</u>, neither shall be."* I ask you, was 70 A.D. worse than the flood?

In Luke 21:22 Jesus states, *"For these be the days of vengeance, <u>that all things which are written may be fulfilled.</u>"* I ask you, has all which was written been fulfilled?

The Quickly Approaching Rapture

In Matthew 24:21 Jesus explains, ***"For then shall be great tribulation, such as was not since the beginning of the world to this time<u>, no, nor ever shall be</u>."*** I ask you, has there been anything worse than the events of 70 A.D. happen in world history since that time?

It's Not New

For those who claim the Rapture is a new doctrine, I hope this book has given you some things to think about. I have laid out some early Church writings that indicate the teaching of the Rapture, or at the very least, the teaching that Jesus could come at any moment for His Church, was, in fact, taught early and is in the Bible.

New Glasses

For those who believe people like me "over-spiritualize" the Bible, my hope and prayer is that you will look at some of the examples I have given about pictures, types and shadows in the Scripture, and that you will look at them with new glasses. I am not asking you to blindly believe, I am asking you to consider the Scriptural evidence I laid out in this book.

Vanished?

For those who have always believed that the Rapture will cause Christians everywhere to simply vanish,

The Quickly Approaching Rapture

I hope you will consider the possibility that our bodies will actually stay behind. I mostly hope that by laying out the two different theories in this book that those during the Tribulation might have a resource that helps them understand what really happened. If we vanish or if our bodies appear to be dead on the streets, I want the person left behind to realize it could still be this thing called the Rapture.

My Prayer

My sincere hope and prayer for anyone reading this book is that no matter what the Rapture looks like or when it occurs, you will have made the right choice.

In Revelation Chapter 3 Verse 20 Jesus tells those who are not His yet, *"Behold, I stand at the door, and knock: if any man hear my voice, and open the door, I will come in to him, and will sup with him, and he with me."*

While this is a letter to the fake Church (Laodicea), which I believe lines up with the Apostasy we are seeing today, Jesus doesn't speak this line to a "church". He speaks it to an individual. He says, *"if any man hear my voice"*, which "man" is the Greek word "Tis" which can mean "any person" (*Strong's* G5100). If "anyone" hears

The Quickly Approaching Rapture

His voice and opens the door, Jesus gives them a promise, *"I will come into him, and sup with him, and he with me"*. What Jesus is saying is that whosoever believes in Him and opens the door, He will come and live within you! He will make you born again and filled with the Oil of the Holy Spirit. You would be wise to answer that door!

Don't Fall Short

In Revelation Chapter 1 the first half of verse 1 is an explanation of the purpose of the book, who wrote it, and when it will occur. It reads, *"The **Revelation of Jesus Christ**, which **God gave unto him**, to shew unto his servants things which **must shortly** come to pass…"*

First, Revelation is all about Jesus. Second, God Himself is responsible for the book. Lastly, the verse gives us the promise that these things *"must shortly come to pass"*.

That last line seems strange to me because John received this letter back in the first century and it certainly hasn't all come to pass yet. So, what's the issue?

Well, there is no issue. First we know what the Scripture says about God fulfilling His promises. In 2 Peter 3 we read, *"But, beloved, be not ignorant of this one thing, that one day is with the Lord as a thousand years, and a thousand years as one day"* (v.8).

So, when you think about it, it has only been a couple days since the first century when it comes to God's timeline.

However, it goes on in verse 9 to say, *"The Lord is not slack concerning his promise, as some men count slackness; but is longsuffering to us-ward, not willing that any should perish, but that all should come to repentance."*

Here we see that the reason God has delayed His coming. He wants any who might be saved, to be saved.

Lastly, in the first part of verse 10 we then see a familiar phrase, *"But the day of the Lord will come as a thief in the night."*

God has a purpose for His timing. He tells us in His Word that He could come at any moment. This is powerful because it motivates us to live righteously because we don't know when He will be here. However, He also encourages us by letting us recognize the signs of His coming so that we could be even more motivated. He then seemingly delays His coming so that, any who might be saved could be saved. Aren't you glad He did so? If He would have

The Quickly Approaching Rapture

come before you and I were saved things would be much different for us. Thank God He waited!

Jumping back to Revelation 1 that phrase that states, *"things which must shortly come to pass"* is actually interesting in regard to timing. The words *"come to pass"* is, according to *Strong's*, a single Greek word, "Ginomai". It can mean, "to cause" or "to become" or "to arise" or "grow" (G1096). So, when we read this passage in Revelation it seems to speak about a time when things will begin to happen and when they do they will grow.

Remember Jesus stated that, *"when these things begin to come to pass, then look up, and lift up your heads; for your redemption draweth nigh"* (Luke 21:28).

So, in the same way I believe the first line in Revelation is saying that when these signs begin to happen they will grow like birth pangs, getting closer together, and have much greater intensity.

Is this what we are seeing around the world today?

We are indeed seeing strange and unexplained events. The pandemic of the Covid-19 "corona virus" is just the latest in a string of "pestilences" that is, the Greek

The Quickly Approaching Rapture

word "Loymos" which means a "plague" or "disease" (G3061). We are seeing strange earthquakes in places not familiar with them. We are seeing strange events like the magnetic north pole moving, strange boom sounds around the world, floods, famines in various nations, wildfires, and certainly wars and rumors of wars are all around us.

We are seeing an Apostasy of the Christian faith in which, a false gospel is being propagated, and stealing millions of converts from hearing the true Gospel of Jesus Christ. This movement seems to be joining with others and we are now seeing the gathering of certain religious elements as the one-world religion appears to be forming.

We have seen the advancement in technology and the ability to have instant world-wide communication and global delivery come about over the last century. We are seeing the move toward a global currency as predicted in Revelation 13, and we are seeing the beginning structure of a one-world government which has been bolstered by this Covid-19 "coronavirus" event.

There is so much happening that was prophesied as happening just before the Tribulation and we are seeing the foundation of things that are prophesied from within the Tribulation. It is clear to me that Jesus will be here soon.

The Quickly Approaching Rapture

While I don't know the day or hour, I most definitely can see the signs!

Again, Luke 21:28 are Jesus' Words, *"And when these things <u>begin</u> to come to pass, then <u>look up</u>, and <u>lift up your heads</u>; for <u>your redemption draweth nigh</u>."*

Jesus Said He's Coming Quickly

In Revelation Chapter 22 Verse 7 Jesus tells us, *"Behold, I come <u>quickly</u>: blessed is he that keepeth the sayings of the prophecy of this book."* In Verse 12 He says something similar, *"And, behold, I come <u>quickly</u>; and my reward is with me, to give every man according as his work shall be."* Then in verse 20 He states, *"He which testifieth these things saith, Surely I come <u>quickly</u>. Amen. Even so, come, Lord Jesus."*

When Jesus says something three times He is highlighting it for a reason. The word used there for "Quickly" three times in Revelation 22 is the Greek word "Tachu". This word, according to *Strong's* means "shortly" or "suddenly" (G5035). This adds to what was said in Revelation Chapter 1 Verse 1 when John was told he was going to be shown things that must *"shortly come to pass"*.

The Quickly Approaching Rapture

These three verses in Revelation 22 are more verses declaring that Jesus Christ could come at any moment for His Church. It will be a sudden event that will shock the world, and He tells us that we will be blessed if we keep *"the sayings of the prophecy of the book"* (v.7). In verse 12 He says He is bringing His reward with Him. In verse 20 He tells us that this is a done deal, ***"He which testifieth these things saith, Surely I come quickly."***

I love how verse 20 ends…
"Even so, come Lord Jesus."
Church He's almost here. He's coming soon.

What If It's Today?

What if the Rapture happens today? Are you ready?
Do you know the Lord?
More importantly, does the Lord know you?

Remember Lot's wife. Her heart was in the world and she perished. Remember Matthew 7 when Jesus tells a whole group of so-called "Christians" that they have to depart from Him because even though they did many works in His Name, Jesus never knew them.

The Quickly Approaching Rapture

Jesus is coming for a faithful Bride. He says the recipe for being faithful is holding to His Word and not denying His name. He tells us to live godly and deny worldly lusts. He warns us to be wise and not foolish. Just like the wise virgins who had the oil, and not like the foolish who didn't.

Get right—or get left.

Chapter 15

Been Left Behind?

What Now?

Whatever just happened, whether a bunch of people just disappeared, seemed to have collapsed dead, or spontaneously combusted, you need to read this Chapter carefully. You have been left behind, but I am going to explain to you how you can still be saved. I will also give you advice on what to do next and some insight to the time-period the world is about to endure.

You may have chosen to do your own thing before the Tribulation, to live your own life, to reject or ignore God's free offer of salvation through Grace, but now that you are in the Tribulation I want you to know a few things. First, I want you to know there is still hope for you. The Gospel of Jesus Christ is valid at any time. We have all sinned and fallen short of the glory of God. The only reason we were taken and you were left, is that we were born-again. What that means is that we surrendered our lives to the King of Kings, Jesus Christ, and received His free offer

The Quickly Approaching Rapture

of Salvation. He then placed His Spirit inside of us and made us worthy. If you remember the story of the Ten Virgins, the oil was the difference. Oil is a picture of the Holy Spirit. We had it, and you didn't. We received His offer of Grace and you ignored it or rejected it. Still, like I said, there is hope for you.

Jesus took all of our sins upon Himself at the Cross. He offers that forgiveness to all. Now that you are in the Tribulation you will not have the luxury that we had prior to this event. We were able to worship the Lord in relative freedom and during much better times. He is still available. He still loves you, and He wants you to believe on Him, repent of your sins, surrender your life to Him and live for Him. If you have a Bible, or if you can get one, here are some key verses to read. First, John 3:16. It reads, *"For God so loved the world, that he gave his only begotten Son, that whosoever believeth in him should not perish, but have everlasting life."*

Ephesians 2:8-9 reads, *"For by grace are ye saved through faith; and that not of yourselves: it is the gift of God: Not of works, lest any man should boast."* Salvation is free. You don't work for it. You simply believe. Acts 16:30-31 tells us as much, *"And brought them out, and said, Sirs, what must I do to be saved? And they said, Believe on the Lord Jesus Christ, and thou shalt be saved, and thy house."* Also, Romans 10:9-10 states, *"That if thou shalt confess with thy mouth the Lord Jesus, and shalt believe in thine heart that God hath raised him from the dead, thou shalt be saved. For with the heart man believeth unto righteousness; and with the mouth confession is made unto salvation."*

If you have that Bible go and read the Book of John and begin to learn about your Savior. Also know that hard times are coming no matter what. If you did just give your life to Jesus from within the tribulation, it may also mean you may have to die for Him. But, and even though this sounds impossible right now, do not worry. God is with you and will see you through this. Place your trust in Him and give Him your whole life! He doesn't say it will be easy, but what He does promise is that it will be worth it!

To My Hebrew Friends

Perhaps you are an Israelite. Maybe you even live in the beautiful nation of Israel. I want you to know that God has amazing things in store for you. If you will simply pick up the book of Isaiah and read Chapter 53 you will realize

The Quickly Approaching Rapture

it's all about Yeshua. In fact, let me just give you that entire Chapter here. But look at the language as you read it. Do you see that the author was inspired to use "past tense" and "present tense" when describing things? This was done for you! It is looking back at what Yeshua did <u>for you</u> and what it means <u>to you</u> in the present.

Isaiah 53 Who hath believed our report? and to whom is the arm of the LORD revealed?² For he shall grow up before him as a tender plant, and as a root out of a dry ground: he hath no form nor comeliness; and when we shall see him, there is no beauty that we should desire him.³ He is despised and rejected of men; a man of sorrows, and acquainted with grief: and <u>we hid as it were our faces from him</u>; he <u>was</u> despised, and <u>we esteemed him not</u>.⁴ Surely he <u>hath borne our griefs, and carried our sorrows: yet we did esteem him stricken, smitten of God, and afflicted.</u>⁵ <u>But he was wounded for our transgressions, he was bruised for our iniquities: the chastisement of our peace was upon him; and with his stripes we are healed.</u>⁶ All we like sheep have gone astray; we have turned everyone to his own way; and the LORD <u>hath laid on him the iniquity of us all.</u>⁷ He <u>was oppressed, and he was afflicted, yet he opened not his mouth: he is brought as a lamb to the slaughter, and as a sheep before her shearers is dumb, so he openeth not his mouth.</u>⁸ <u>He was taken from prison and from judgment: and who shall declare his generation? for he was cut off out of the land of the living: for the transgression of my people was he stricken.</u>⁹ <u>And he made his grave with the wicked, and with the rich in his death; because he had done no violence, neither was any deceit in his mouth.</u>¹⁰ Yet it pleased the LORD to bruise him; he hath put him to grief: when thou shalt make his soul an offering for sin, he shall see his seed, he shall prolong his days, and the pleasure of the LORD shall prosper in his hand.¹¹ He shall see of the travail of his soul, and shall be satisfied: by his knowledge shall my righteous servant justify many; for he shall bear their iniquities.¹² Therefore will I divide him a portion with the great, and he shall divide the spoil with the strong; because he hath poured out his

The Quickly Approaching Rapture

soul unto death: and he was numbered with the transgressors; <u>and he bare the sin of many, and made intercession for the transgressors.</u>

The Outline of the Tribulation to Come

Whether you believe or don't believe in Yeshua at this moment I also want to give you an idea of what you can expect now that you find yourself in the Tribulation. First, as mentioned, something just happened. A massive number of people disappeared, appeared to die—or whatever. The World is in chaos and people are freaking out. You are scared, and everyone around you has a theory. Some are sure it was aliens; some think it was the planet protecting itself, some think it was a pandemic, others think it was a biological weapon, and some are claiming it was the Rapture. Well, it was the Rapture. But know this, a group of leaders are going to begin to work together. Among them will be one strong leader that seems to bring comfort and ease with his words. He will be aided by a religious leader, most likely who calls himself a Christian, but you will notice he is working with several religions to bring peace among chaos.

All of these people are going to tell you there is nothing to fear. They may even give you some kind of reason for the "sudden death", "disappearance" or whatever

The Quickly Approaching Rapture

just happened to all those people. There will be some among them who assure you it wasn't this "Rapture" thing, after all, look at all the "Christian" leaders on the stage or who are still with us. After all, the religious leader himself is still here and he has a message for you. Also, they may offer you the "cure" for what has killed or zapped millions. They may even offer you free money in the form of digital currency to get you through the hard times. There will be a parade of world leaders and celebrities and important people telling you that there is nothing to fear. Come get your money, your cure, your vaccine, your chip implanted. You will be okay.

A word of advice, don't take anything they have to offer. Your soul depends on it.

As mentioned, among this group of what appears to be ten nations there will be a leader that comes to the forefront to help them. He is charismatic, charming, and he is able to do things no one else has ever done. He is aided by this religious leader, and the world is in awe of him.

White Horse

This leader moves to a place of power and prominence on a platform of peace (Rev 6:1-2). The world heralds him as some kind of messiah. In fact, many in

The Quickly Approaching Rapture

Israel and perhaps even in Arab nations will begin to believe he is the "promised one". He is so good that he is able to broker peace in the middle east. He swings a deal with Israel and the Palestinians and affirms a covenant with Israel. He allows Israel to rebuild a Temple and begin their religious sacrifices once again. The world is in absolute awe of his tactics, his smooth words, and the signs and miracles he is able to do. They follow him faithfully.

This "leader" then creates a monetary system in which, everyone will have to receive a "mark" which consists of a name or a number related to him and his kingdom. This is often called the "Mark of the Beast". If you go read Revelation Chapter 13 it is all in there. And, if you take this mark in the form or a "name" or a "number" you will also be forfeiting your soul. DO NOT TAKE THIS MARK!

Red Horse

We also know that this diabolical leader will then start a war, or cause others to do so (Rev 6:3-4). This will be a horrible bloody war. Although we are not sure about the timing of everything we do know that this leader is going to defeat three of the world leaders in some way (Dan 3:8), but we also know that this evil dictator will suffer a head wound of some kind (Rev 13:3). The world will be captivated by what transpires. This dictator survives, or appears to resurrect from the dead, and when he does he comes back stronger than before.

Black and Pale Horses

Following the horrible war there will be a time of brutal famine on the planet (Rev 6:5-6), and this will be followed by a lot of death and decay (Rev 6:7-8). We also know this evil man is going to declare himself to be god and desecrate the newly built Jewish Temple. The Jews will reject him at that point and he will turn on them and seek to destroy them. He is also going to kill many others who become believers in Jesus Christ at the time as well (Rev 6:9-11). If you have just become a believer in Jesus, this is where you may have to give your life up rather than worship this evil satanic inspired leader. But, do not fear, Jesus Christ will give you the courage and ability to get through it.

The Deadly Trio

Still, there are other challenges ahead for those who survive. Following the war, famine, pestilence, and death, events that are even more fearful begin to occur. As previously mentioned large hail stones will fall on the Earth

The Quickly Approaching Rapture

(Rev 8:7), followed by a *"great mountain burning"* which hits the Earth and devastates the seas. After this another *"great star"* called *"Wormwood"* will hit the planet and make bitter much of the world's fresh water supply. We know these three things will cause the light of the sun and moon to diminish greatly and the Earth to stagger like a drunk man. Which, could indicate a removal from its natural orbit or rotation.

Locusts

Following those events something that we don't really understand happens. God allows the *"bottomless pit"* to be opened and from it comes smoke like a *"great furnace"* (Rev 9:2). Out of this smoke comes something that is described as *"locusts"* but they are not like any locusts we have ever seen. These have *"power"* as *"scorpions"* and they don't eat grass or the trees. Instead they are commanded to hurt those who do not have the *"Seal of God"* in their foreheads (Rev 9:4). These locusts are then able to *"torment"* non-believers for *"five months"* (Rev 9:5). It then says in Revelation 9:6 that, *"In those days shall men seek death, and shall not find it; and shall to desire to die and shall flee from them."* We don't know what these things are, but a full description is found in

The Quickly Approaching Rapture

Revelation 9:8-10 and in verse 11 the Bible says that these locusts have a king named *"Abaddon"* in Hebrew or *"Apollyon"* in Greek which both mean *"Destroyer"* or *"Destroying Angel"*.

It is my personal opinion that whatever these things are they are demonic in origin. They could be fallen angels or some other kind of entity, but whatever they are they are led by one called the Destroying Angel.

200,000,000 Soldiers

During the chaos more war will occur. At this time an army of two-hundred million will advance on the Middle East. However, this army also has a strange description. Some have claimed it would be Chinese armies, some say it will be made up of Muslim nations. I just don't know. What I do know is they have a strange description. Some think it is describing modern war machines in first century language, but again, I just don't know. In Revelation 9:17-19 we read, *"And thus I saw the horses in the vision, and them that sat on them, having breastplates of fire, and of jacinth, and brimstone: and <u>the heads of the horses were as the heads of lions</u>; and out of <u>their mouths issued fire and smoke and brimstone</u>. By these three was the third part of men killed, by the fire,* *and by the smoke, and by the brimstone, which issued out of their mouths. For their power is in their mouth, and in their tails: for their tails were like unto serpents, and had heads, and with them they do hurt."*

The sad thing is that at the end of Revelation 9 we read that despite all the world is going through many people still refuse to repent. Verses 20-21 states, *"And <u>the rest of the men which were not killed by these plagues yet repented not of the works of their hands</u>, that they should not worship devils, and idols of gold, and silver, and brass, and stone, and of wood: which neither can see, nor hear, nor walk: <u>Neither repented they of their murders, nor of their sorceries, nor of their fornication, nor of their thefts</u>."*

The Image of the Beast

Another thing for you to understand is that at some point during the Tribulation this evil leader, who we know is in fact the Anti-Christ, will set up a system of commerce as previously noted. He will require all who wish to buy or sell obtain a *"mark"* in their right hands or their foreheads (Rev 13:16). He is also going to create some kind of *"Image"* that will appear to be alive in some way. My guess is that it is some kind of artificial intelligence tied

The Quickly Approaching Rapture

into a global network connected to something that is robotic in nature, but make no mistake, the Bible says it will have some form of "life" within itself.

I wrote about all of this in my book *Mark(s) of the Beast*, but you can study this more by looking at Revelation 13 closely. Whatever this thing is the whole world will be forced to worship it—or else.

Grievous Sores

In Revelation 16 we read that everyone who does receive the *"name of the beast"* or the *"number of his name"* and worship the *"image of the beast"* will also develop some kind of *"grievous sore"* on their bodies (Rev 16:2).

Blood of a Dead Man

At this same time the environment will continue to get worse. True climate change will be in full swing and the Bible says the sea will become like the *"blood of a dead man"* and that everything in it will die (Rev 16:3). Everything....

Sun Burn

Revelation 16:8 explains that the sun will burn like never before. It reads, *"And the fourth angel poured out his vial upon the sun; and power was given unto him to scorch men with fire."*

It then states in the very next verse that people still don't repent, *"And men were scorched with great heat, and blasphemed the name of God, which hath power over these plagues: and they repented not to give him glory."*

Darkness

The Bible then describes a time when darkness would come upon the kingdom of the beast (Rev 16:11). They continue to blaspheme God (v.11). This makes me wonder how the sun becomes so bright but then darkness occurs. I guess it's possible that something large could actually hit the sun causing it to suffer great explosions and then diminish some. But, please know, that's just my own speculation.

Kings of the East

The Bible explains that during this time of darkness the River Euphrates dries up so that, *"the kings of the east might be prepared"* (v.12). Some believe this is that same 200,000,000 soldier army written about in Chapter 9, but I don't know. All I know is more forces are moving into place for a final conflict.

Armageddon

The Quickly Approaching Rapture

All of this leads up to a gathering of many armies in Israel in a place called *"Armageddon"* (Rev 16:16). However, a huge earthquake stops the battle before it can happen (Rev 16:18) and *"every island fled away"* and *"the mountains were not found"* and once again *"great hail out of heaven"* falls upon the Earth (Rev 16:21).

Babylon

We know at this time God is going to continue to pour out His wrath on the world, but in particular, a place the Scripture calls Babylon, or as Revelation 17:5 describes it, *"Mystery, Babylon The Great, The Mother Of Harlots And Abominations Of The Earth"*. This is most likely the headquarters of the kingdom of the Anti-Christ, but within that kingdom is the source of the evil false one-world government and economy and the horrible blasphemous evil one-world religion. I could say more, but I won't. However, you should be able to recognize this from inside of the Tribulation.

Here He Comes

At this time, if you are able to live through all I have just described in minimal detail, you will see Jesus coming in the clouds and we will be with Him! Revelation 19:11-14 states, *"And I saw heaven opened, and behold a*

The Quickly Approaching Rapture

white horse; and he that sat upon him was called Faithful and True, and in righteousness he doth judge and make war. His eyes were as a flame of fire, and on his head were many crowns; and he had a name written, that no man knew, but he himself. And he was clothed with a vesture dipped in blood: and his name is called The Word of God. And the armies which were in heaven followed him upon white horses, clothed in fine linen, white and clean."

Again, if you are reading this book from within the time known as the Tribulation just know you can still be saved. This is only true if you haven't bowed your knee to the Anti-Christ and received his mark. If you haven't, and you are now living for Jesus, just know, you may also have to die for Jesus. If you make it through the Tribulation you will see Him coming in the clouds. He will then set up His Kingdom on Earth for 1,000 literal years, and you will be part of that. I hope and pray that you made the right choice.

Now, if you are reading this before the Tribulation and you haven't received Christ, what in the world are you waiting for!?

The End... is Near

Study Resources

These are some of my recommendations

Feel free to contact me:thoughtfulapologetics@yahoo.com

YouTube, Television - Radio or Internet Sites

HisChannel: www.hischannel.com

CSN Radio: https://csnradio.com/

Discover the Book Ministries: www.discoverthebook.org
YouTube Channel- *DTBM*

Greg Laurie: https://harvest.org/
YouTube Channel- *Pastor Greg Laurie*

Jon Courson: https://joncourson.com/
YouTube Channel- *Searchlight with Jon Courson*

Chuck Smith: https://calvarychapel.com/pastorchuck/twft
YouTube Channel- *Chuck Smith TWFT*

Skip Heitzig: https://connectwithskip.com/
YouTube Channel- *Calvary Church with Skip Heitzig*

The Quickly Approaching Rapture

Dr. Charles Stanley: www.intouch.org
YouTube Channel- *In Touch Ministries*

Tony Clark: https://www.calvarynn.church/

Ray Comfort: https://www.livingwaters.com/
YouTube Channel – *Living Waters*

David Rosales: https://calvaryccv.org/
YouTube Channel- *Calvary Chapel Chino Valley*

Dr. Ed Hindson: www.thekingiscoming.com
YouTube Channel- *Dr. Ed Hindson*

Ravi Zacharias: https://www.rzim.org/
YouTube Channel- *Ravi Zacharias International Ministries*

Jack Hibbs: https://reallifewithjackhibbs.org/
YouTube Channel- *Real Life with Jack Hibbs*

Raul Ries: www.somebodylovesyou.com
YouTube Channel- *Somebody Loves You Worldwide*

The Quickly Approaching Rapture

Here is a list of even more resources.
You can search for them on the web or on YouTube.
Always Be Ready (https://alwaysbeready.com/)
Blue Letter Bible (www.blueletterbible.org)
E-Sword Bible (www.e-sword.net)
Ken Graves (GodSword)
Mike MacIntosh (HisChannel)
Barry Stagner (HisChannel)
Amir Tsarfati (Behold Israel)
Don Stewart (HisChannel)
Alistair Begg (Truth for Life)
Dr. David Jeremiah
Jan Markell (Understanding the Times)
Wretched Radio with Todd Friel
D. James Kennedy
John MacArthur (Grace to You)
Koinonia House (Chuck Missler)
David Guzik (Enduring Word)
Pancho Juarez
Dave Rolph (The Balanced Word)
Hal Lindsey (HisChannel)
Donald Perkins (HisChannel)

The Quickly Approaching Rapture

[i] All Scripture quoted is from the King James Version of the Holy Bible unless otherwise noted.

[ii] Walter C. Kaiser, *An Introduction to Biblical Hermeneutics: the Search for Meaning*, (Grand Rapids, MI: Zondervan, 2007), kl172.

[iii] *Things to Come: A Study in Biblical Eschatology*, (Grand Rapids: MI, Zondervan, 1964), kl105.

[iv] Ibid., kl107.

[v] Jon Courson, *Jon Courson's Application Commentary: New Testament*, (Nashville, TN: Thomas Nelson Publishers, 2003), kl623.

[vi] Chuck Smith, *What the World is Coming To*, (Costa Mesa, CA: Word for Today, 2001), kl1065.

[vii] Ibid., kl1076.

[viii] *Didache*, Chapter 16 n.d.

[ix] Ibid., Ch 16.

[x] Ibid., Ch 16.

[xi] Don Stewart, *The Rapture An Introduction to the Blessed Hope of the Church*, (San Dimas, CA: Educating the World, 2016), p.188.

[xii] Lightfoot, J.B., trans. "Early Christian Writings: New Testament, Apocrypha, Gnostics, Church Fathers." *The Shepherd of Hermas*. http://www.earlychristianwritings.com/text/shepherd-lightfoot.html. 2[23]:1.

[xiii] Ibid., 2[23]:4

[xiv] Ibid., 2[23]:5

[xv] *Victorinus, Saint. Commentary on the Apocalypse .Unknown.* Kindle Edition. Ch.15 V.1

[xvi] Ibid., Ch.6 V.14.

[xvii] Nelson, Arthur. "Flooding and Heavy Rains Rise 50% Worldwide in a Decade, Figures Show ." The Guardian. Guardian News and Media,March21,2018.

The Quickly Approaching Rapture

https://www.theguardian.com/environment/2018/mar/21/flooding-and-heavy-rains-rise-50-worldwide-in-a-decade-figures-show.

[xviii] "Facts Statistics: Wildfires." Insurance Information Institute. AccessedJanuary2020.https://www.iii.org/fact-statistic/facts-statistics-wildfires.

[xix] Woodward, Aylin. "Earth's Magnetic North Pole Is Skittering Wildly across the Arctic. By 2040, Our Compasses 'Will Point Eastward of True North,' an Expert Says." Business Insider. Business-Insider,-December-22,-2019. https://www.businessinsider.com/magnetic-north-moving-wildly-compass-problem-2019-12.

[xx] "NASA Solar System Exploration." NASA Science. NASA, August 31,2018.https://solarsystem.nasa.gov/planets/hypothetical-planet-x/in-depth/.

Made in the USA
Columbia, SC
29 May 2021